MW00916706

The Everyday Miracles Series

Gems from God's Operators Manual

EVERYDAY MIRACLES

Manifesting the More Abundant Life

by GOD'S DESIGN

Dr. David A. Jernigan

ACKNOWLEDGEMENTS

I would like to express my profound thanks
to my wife and soul mate, whose
love, knowledge, patience, and friendship
sustain me while I continue to grow.

Special thanks and appreciation go to
Dr. Samantha Joseph, my great friend and
practice partner, whose knowledge and
pure heart of God's love brought
much clarity to the topics in this book.
I would also like to give heartfelt thanks
to Katy Penner, whose editorial help has
made reading this book more enjoyable for all.
Special thanks also to the many friends
who critiqued the earlier edits.
A part of all of you is in this book!

DEDICATED TO MY PARENTS,
ROBERT AND MONA JERNIGAN;
WHO CONTINUE TO KNOW NO BOUNDS IN THEIR LIVING
TESTIMONY FOR GOD,
AND WHO TAUGHT ME FROM BIRTH TO LOVE GOD,
RESPECT HIS WORD
AND TO
EXPECT EVERYDAY MIRACLES.

CONTENTS

PREFACE

The inspiration for this book arose from a sense of knowingness that everyone on the planet needs to be empowered with the knowledge that God's Word is true and that the latest scientific endeavors are continually reaffirming this fact! What I know to be true is that as my family, and others with whom we have shared this knowledge, practice the truths laid forth in this book, the miracles are stacking up. From the complete healing of my eleven-year-old daughter's paralysis of both legs from West Nile Virus, to instantaneously fixing broken computers, printers and automobiles we are finding the "little miracles" are becoming commonplace and too numerous to recall. Only the "bigger ones" remain in memory – although we thank God for all blessings big and small.

All of us are on a journey that has no end, but with the correct destination, the journey is empowering the farther along we go. *Everyday Miracles by God's Design* is not the end all dissertations on how to manifest the miraculous, "more than abundant life" promised us by God. It is a guide.

I believe the contents of this book are divinely inspired! I am not a theologian trained in hallowed halls of stone and brick. I am what the Word of God says I am...a worthy Son of God, heir to all that God is and joint-heir with Christ.

Open your mind and heart to what God is saying. I have purposely focused this book on God's light and love. You will find no "fire and brimstone" because I want and God wants for you to operate in His "perfect love" without fear and without condemnation. If you will walk in the light as God is in the light, a tremendous miracle will happen... all fear will evaporate.

Great efforts were made to accurately interpret God's Word throughout this book, based upon the ancient and original text of the Holy Bible, the prior usage of the words, the context of the reference, and most importantly by opening my heart and mind and simply asking God to show me and teach me His truth.

I have provided the scripture references in the body of the text so that you can immediately see that what I am saying is backed up by God's Word in the Bible.

Each time I read this book, I am overwhelmed by the light of God's love to everyone emanating from the text. It was never hidden, but the real "how to" of living a miracle-filled life is revealed here again in God's words to you.

This book is short enough to read virtually every day. I encourage you to work the concepts in this book by purposely and consciously taking it apart piece by piece and meditating on it. Integrate each aspect into every moment of every day. Your ultimate goal should be to master all of the principles presented in this book.

What we know is that God's Word has a mathematical and scientific precision. To leave out anything is to destroy this precision. As you practice these keys presented herein, you will find that God will develop in you a sense of "know-ingness" so you can always know, beyond the ability of your five senses to know, when you are de-powering Him in your life. Cultivate this knowingness and you will know what works and what is required for you to manifest God's power in your life through signs, miracles and wonders.

Everyday Miracles by God's Design is written to and for all, from no particular religious denomination or theology other than being based upon the right-use-ness (right applica-tion to righteousness) of God's Word, referenced through The Holy Bible. It is a path that all can follow who seek to know God better. It is also a guide to reaching our highest level of spiritual achievement (the Greek word, *teleioteta*), meaning "perfection," as spoken of in Mark 6:1 - perfect love.

I am so excited for you! Read it a hundred times if neces-sary and be empowered with God's light and love.

I pray that the eyes of your understanding be enlightened and that your heart be empowered with the knowledge that your highest calling is to reach ever greater spiritual matu-rity as a child of God.

May God be glorified in this work.

—*David A. Jernigan*

1

FOUNDATIONAL TRUTHS, GREAT REWARDS

Let this mind be in you which was also in Christ Jesus!
(Phil. 2:5)

Blessings to you on this day! I hope as you read that you are in a relaxed state of mind and body. I want to share with you that there exists the very real possibility for miracles to be an everyday event in your life. When you realize just how much control you have over life, you will cease to be a victim of circumstance.

Before we get too far into this topic, we must come to a foundational agreement. This book's frame of reference is the Bible. Interestingly, many of the truths in the Bible are also found, almost verbatim, in the other great religions of the world. If we want to manifest everyday miracles in our own lives (either physical, emotional, or spiritual healing), or if we want to tap the resources of God for the "more than abundant life," then these universal truths must be understood, accepted, and implemented.

The concepts of this book strive to present only "universal truths." Religious and denominational bigotry, the lack of love and appreciation for God's one body, is the poison of the world (1 Corinthians 12:14).

In order for you to fully apply the principles in this book, you must replace the resentment, hate, and fear with God's greatest commandment, "You must love the Lord thy God with all your heart, mind, soul, and strength and love your neighbor as yourself" (Luke 10:27). Notice it didn't say to love your "Christian neighbor," nor the "People of your belief system." It said, "Your neighbor." That is our neighbor living in the house next door; the neighbor across town; the neighboring town; the neighboring state; the neighboring country! This is the example given in Luke 10:30-37 of the "Good Samaritan." The point of the story of the Good Samaritan was that the Samaritan, who was of a different country and belief system, took compassion on the man from Jerusalem, who had been robbed and beaten and left "half dead" by thieves while on his way to Jericho. The Samaritan bound up his wounds and poured on essential oils and wine, placed him on his horse, cared for him at an inn, and upon departing the inn the next day he gave the innkeeper money saying, "Take care of him; and if you must spend more than this in the caring of him, then I will repay you when I come back through this area."

In a nutshell, we are called by the universal truth to "Be love" (1 John 4:7-8). We are to walk in a perpetual state of God's love. We are to walk in a constantly and purposely sustained state of heart that Jesus demonstrated. Jesus stated, "I and my Father are one." We are encouraged in the Bible to purposely put on this same mindset or consciousness of Christ Jesus (Eph. 1:19). So, you must strive to maintain this same mindset that Jesus has, and know with a certainty and be able to say from your heart that "I and my heavenly Father are one." You are in perfect alignment as a child of God. When you have this consciousness and you actively decide to completely turn away from all of the thoughts, words, and deeds which are not in alignment with God's love for all things, then you will open up God's power to work in and through you in everyday miracles.

Many people fail to manifest a more than abundant life because the Bible is not real to them. They do not realize God's Word is alive and dynamic! God is the same yesterday, today, and forever (Heb. 13:8). We must change our thinking if we are stuck in a three-dimensional mentality, believing that the physical world is all that exists, with God being some ambiguous energy somewhere out there. God is real! Innumerable miracles do happen daily as real people successfully cultivate greater knowledge and understanding of God's light and love.

To see God's power manifesting through you as everyday miracles, you must actively pursue God's truths with all of your heart, mind, soul and strength.

Because of this, our foundation for learning how to access everyday miracles is based upon the absolute acceptance that the Word of God is the Will of God. If you want to truly know what God's Will is for you and your life, you must know and believe His Word. You will see later why this is so very important when it comes to loving God, trusting God, and having faith in God.

A hindrance to everyday miracles is that everyone looks at the lives of the people around them and sees only mutual misery. When disease becomes the norm, most accept the disease as their lot in life by saying, "Why should I strive for anything else?"

You must separate yourself from what the world says is normal and align all that you are to what God says is true (Romans 12:2).

Pretend, if you must, that you are the only one in the world who "really gets it," and take the leap of faith to really live every moment of every day completely immersed in God's truth, light, and love. Make it your highest priority, your highest calling in life.

Now, let's learn how to tap the promised and unlimited resources of God so that you can instantly manifest everyday miracles!

You can manifest everyday miracles when you consciously and purposely move God's light, love, and truths from simply being head knowledge to creative heart knowledge.

You can manifest everyday miracles when you consciously and purposely move God's light, love, and truths from simply being head knowledge to creative heart knowledge.

What everyday miracles can you expect? Do you recall at the start of this, we agreed to believe God's Word to be perfect and true, and that it details His absolute will or desire for you? Philippians 4:19 tells us part of His desire towards you: "God will supply all your needs according to His power and for His glory, through Christ in you." So it doesn't matter whether you need food, something to drink, new clothes, or anything at all.

If you will stay focused on God's truths and seek God's love, continually building His Temple within you, Matthew 6:33 says all your needs will be provided. As you have need, and as you have consistently walked in God's light and love, allowing God to work in and through you, you will be able to heal without scars, to change physical matter (such as turn water into wine and to walk on water), to provide food and sustenance at will, and to calm the strongest hurricane. Yet one of the greatest miracles will also be yours to experience: a heart of joy, peace, contentment and happiness that surpasses all understanding.

The world we live in appreciates science, and it accepts that the technology that science has brought into our lives is based upon laws of science. These laws are what make your TV or CD player work every time you turn them on. So too, prayer works on fixed laws of God.

Do you want to manifest a loaf of bread when you are hungry? Do you want to disperse a hurricane? Do you want to heal the sick and broken hearted? Then you must learn to operate the technology of God. God's Word, the "Operator's Manual" for the universe, explains this law of receiving: whatever you desire, when you pray, believe with no doubt in your heart that you will receive it, and you will have your desire. But, when you pray for your desire, pray forgiveness to anyone you have a problem with, so that God will forgive you and see you as spiritually clean (Mark 11:24-26 expanded translation). If you don't receive your desire, then you have asked amiss and the problem is with you, not with God (James 4:3). You may be wondering what things are considered amiss. The "anything you desire" part of this law is predicated by the law that deals with our thinking. You can be assured that you are not praying "amiss" when you are thinking only those things that are true, right, honest, of good report, pure, admirable, praiseworthy, and lovely (Phil. 4:8). Asking amiss would be praying to receive something that glorifies you instead of God, such as miraculously manifesting a loaf of bread as a bar trick to dazzle people. Asking amiss would also be anything that is simply to satisfy your material lusts.

The law of receiving and manifesting everyday miracles operates perfectly when we are in sustained, perfect atonement with God. This atonement and the explanation of the laws of receiving are best defined by B. T. Spalding:

> *The law of receiving and manifesting everyday miracles operates perfectly when we are in sustained, perfect atonement with God.*

"The secret lies in getting the at-one-ment (atonement with God); getting the consciousness of it and then holding firmly and never deviating, though all the earth should oppose. 'Of myself I can do nothing,' said Jesus, 'The Father that dwells in me, He does the work.' Have faith in God. Have faith and doubt not. Have faith and fear not. Now remember there is no limitation to God's power. 'All things are possible to them that believe.'

Use positive words in making your request. There is naught but the perfect condition desired. Then plant in your soul the perfect seed idea and that alone. Now ask to manifest health and not to be healed of disease; to express harmony and realize abundance – not to be delivered from disharmony, misery and limitations. Throw these off as you would an old garment. They are old and only outgrown things; you can afford to discard them joyfully. Do not even turn to gaze at them. They are no thing – nothing.

Fill the seemingly blank spaces about you with the thought of God, Infinite Good. Then remember the word, God, is a seed. It must grow.

Leave the how, when, and where to God. Your work is merely to say what you want and to give forth blessings, knowing that the moment you have asked, you have received. All the details of this "bringing forth" are the work of the Father. Remember, He does the work. Do faithfully your part; leave and trust God's part to Him. Ask. Affirm. Look to God for what you want; then receive God's fulfillment.

Keep the thought of God's abundance always in mind. If any other thought comes, replace it with that of God's abundance and bless that abundance. Give thanks constantly, if need be, that the work is done. Do not go back again to the asking."

Manifesting everyday miracles does not require you to pray for specific needs. As you express God's love through you to the world around you, the world around you will return God's love back to you...this is God's grace (2 Cor. 9:8, Gal. 5:22-23).

Notice that none of these everyday miracles are created by our intensely focused thinking or our good works. It is only through the mighty power of God. As He is one with us, we continually, and joyfully, operate in the renewed mind of Christ (*Christ* here in the original text is the word *Christos*. Christos is a verb, not a noun, and refers to the *anointing* in us of God's applied love, instead of a shortened name for Christ Jesus the son of God) and see His power manifested in and through us (Psalms 37:4-5 and 1 Cor. 2:16).

Operating "in the renewed mind of Christ," or what we sometimes call "living in Christ-consciousness," is when we are living and thinking with the sole purpose to be as clean of body, mind, and spirit, as we can, in order to truly know and be one with our heavenly Father.

Notice that none of these everyday miracles are created by our intensely focused thinking or our good works.

Jesus said, "If you abide in me and my words abide in you, you can ask what you will and it will be done, herein is my Father glorified, that you bear much fruit" (John 15:7). Everyday miracles! You will see it when you believe it! You will see it when you know it to be true!

While miracles do not happen as a result of intensely focusing our brain power, they do require faith in God to do the work. Faith is not a situation where you "try" to believe. Faith is the product of love (Galatians 5:6). Faith works because of love. Love is our greatest calling. When Jesus was asked what the greatest commandment is, he replied, "To love the Lord thy God with all your heart, mind, soul, and with all your strength." To actually be the embodiment of God's love is what life is all about. Grow and purposely cultivate your ability to truly love God, yourself, and everything and everyone God has made, and your faith in Him will grow from a mustard seed to a huge coconut (the world's largest seed)! In Matthew 17:20-21 Jesus said, "If you have faith [the product of love] as a mustard seed [a very small seed, about the size of a pinhead], you can say to a mountain, 'Move from here and go over there;' and it will move; <u>and nothing will be impossible for you</u>." Jesus goes on in the next verse to say exactly what is required to really be able to do a miracle such as moving a mountain. He says, "However, this kind of miracle will not happen without much prayer and fasting." Here we see a true gem of "how to" build our ability to love, by much prayer and fasting. Fasting is the voluntary abstinence from food for a period of time.

So, if you want more faith to produce everyday miracles, you must build it through much prayer, which always involves meditation. It may help you to understand this to see prayer as the transmitter and meditation as the receiver. Meditation is multipurpose. It can be the listening part of having prayed. It can also be the focusing all that you are upon a concept until enlightenment is realized. It is natural that if you ask a question of anyone, including God, you would listen for an answer. Focus all that you are – your head brain, your heart brain, your entire being – towards quietly listening and/or deeply considering, from all angles, the needs and desires you have prayed about. We will go into greater detail concerning meditation in a later chapter.

In prayer you let your needs be known unto God, remembering to pray as B.T. Spalding earlier so eloquently said, "...ask to manifest health and not to be healed of disease; to express harmony and realize abundance – not to be delivered from disharmony, misery and limitations." In other words, don't pray the ineffectual prayer we were all taught, "Dear God, please fix this or that problem" or "Dear God, please help me get this or that done." Instead see yourself as who you truly are, an absolutely powerful child of God. Pray with the knowingness that it is the "Christ in you" to whom you are praying. Eliminate the thoughts of separation between yourself and God, and be one with God, even as Jesus said "I and my Father are one" (John 10:30). Pray now, that you may more completely magnify and amplify the Christ-light and love in you towards the end result that you desire. If you will but step up to the reality of who you are in this universe as a son or daughter of God, invincible by design, you will cease to ask God to do things for you and start speaking your desires into being. Phil. 4:13 says, "I can do all things through Christ [consciousness in action] which strengthens me." Most people read this as Jesus somehow giving them the strength to do all things or anything. But this is not what it is saying! Once again we must go back and remember that the word Christ is the Greek word *Christos* in the original text, which is a verb, not a noun, and not a shortened name for Jesus Christ. When the Bible says, "Christ Jesus" in the original texts, it always said "Christos Iesous." It is important to make this concept heart knowledge. This verse says exactly what it means. You can do all things through Christ, *Christos* (verb, the anointing of God's light and love) which (not "who" strengthens me, further support that the use of the word Christ here is not referring to a person, but an empowering energy of God) strengthens you. Take your power! Speak signs, miracles, and wonders into being by accepting Christ/*Christos* as your divine, empowering, anointing as a true child of God!

Scientifically speaking, Christos is way beyond the eleven dimensions being postulated by today's leading physicists. Even time is being recognized as a linear dimension on the same order as physical matter. If you live life thinking all that exists is the physical universe and that physical matter follows rigid laws, then you haven't been paying attention to the latest scientific research that absolutely reveals that nothing in our world operates on the rigid laws of physics. What you perceive as reality is largely determined by what you hold to be true in your heart.

Let me give you an example of how physical matter and everyday miracles are made of Christos. First, Genesis 1:3 says that on the first day God created light, but later in verse fourteen God created light again in the form of photons, identifying the sun, moon, and stars as the source of the later. What was the first light God created? It was this Christos, God's light and love that permeates all of God's creations in the universe! This first light is separate from the three-dimensional universe of land, air, sea, and galaxies, yet it is in all and through all (Eph. 4:6; Col. 3:11). This Christos is the "God-substance" that makes up all miracles, knowledge, and wisdom (Col. 2:2-3).

My family experienced the reality of playing by God's rules when my oldest daughter, who was ten years old at the time, contracted West Nile Virus. Through a series of unfortunate events, the condition remained inaccurately diagnosed until she was in dire straits. I had, from the start of symptoms, been addressing her condition with confidence that her body would perform as it should with the thoughtfully applied treatments and therapies. By the end of the first week, we realized she was really in trouble and upon retesting her, determined the West Nile virus was the culprit. By this time, she was in excruciating pain, screaming that it felt like her legs were broken at the top of her thigh bones. She said it felt like they had been put through a pencil sharpener. No comfort could be found in any position. The bedcovers being moved elicited screams of agony. We all prayed earnestly for a miracle as I worked day and night to come up with a cure on the physical plane. It was useless to hospitalize her since the medical doctors were saying there was no help for this condition. I used every treatment and therapy in my great arsenal of healing tools from my clinic (one of America's best-equipped healing centers), all to no avail. After weeks of agony, I realized that her body temperature was hovering around 99-100.3°F, not high enough to be of any healing benefit. Recognizing this marked a turning point in her symptoms. With repeated doses of a homeopathic remedy called Hepar Sulf 6x given every fifteen minutes, her body temperature mechanisms were supported until her temperature reached 102.5°F, the optimal body temperature for enabling the body to correctly respond to infections. In near-miraculous fashion, in the hour it took to reach 102.5°F, all the pain completely disappeared! This was a tremendous relief; however, our joy was short-lived. What we found underneath all the pain was the worst possible effect of West Nile – flaccid paralysis of both legs from the destruction of the motor cells in the spinal cord. All of the news media had been reporting that the flaccid paralysis is irreversible, and our hearts sank at the prospect of this beautiful young life subjected to a lifetime in a wheelchair.

You may be wondering where our miraculous God-abilities were during this ordeal. I can assure you we definitely were praying and speaking our intent of complete restoration throughout. Only in hindsight can I tell you why our prayers were ineffective. One day, I walked into the room where she lay. I picked her up, carrying her into the room next door where we had a treatment table set up. As I laid her frail-looking body on the table, I began checking all of her leg muscles for any sign of impulse. There was not even a detectible quiver or twitch in any muscle when I asked her to resist my pushing and pulling of isolated muscles. The three-dimensional body's physical tissues had been destroyed by the virus, and none of the best treatments I had could restore what she had lost.

We had already gone through great pain, and we had all learned much through the ordeal that helped us grow mentally, emotionally, and spiritually. I took her to the room with the treatment table with the idea that I had to do something, but what? Upon completing my test of her leg muscles, I suddenly had a peace in my heart. She lay there on the table and looked up at me with such love that I knew she also had a peace about her. As I stood there looking down at her, I knew what we needed to do. I said to her, "It is time for us to take our spiritual authority over this!" She smiled and said,

"Yes, it is!" I proceeded to pray out loud, instructing her to say what I said, "Dear Heavenly Father, we acknowledge you in all that we are about to do and say. I now clean this vessel and make it sacred and pure with your light and love. I give this body permission to function perfectly on all levels in spite of our past fears and in spite of the damage this virus caused. We speak perfect restoration to all tissues, enabling your light and love to permeate and heal all now, and we make it so now as your children. For your praise and so that you may be glorified, Father."

Upon completing this simple prayer, I lifted her leg with complete peace and pushed against her quadriceps muscles…they instantly held a strong contraction, as did all the other muscles of both legs! With mutual shouts of joy and the most beautiful smile, she gave me a high-five! With tears in my eyes, I told her, "Don't you ever let anyone steal from you what just happened here! God's light and love has healed you!"

You may be wondering why the earlier prayers didn't work. You may also be wondering how spiritual means can restore physical tissue. Hopefully in this later question you now comprehend that Christos permeates all things, even virally destroyed spinal cords. The earlier prayers I now realize didn't work because they were the "freaked-out" prayers of worried parents and children. The prayer that finally worked was spoken from the heart with no fear, meaning we both were operating according to God's design – in His love, unchanged by our outward circumstance!

Everyday miracles are the working of Christos in every dimension by the correctly oriented heart of love. The physics of science is now realizing this truth more and more. A great example of this expansion of our concepts of reality is seen in shows and movie documentaries like *What the Bleep do we Know?* and *The Elegant Universe*, produced by Nova.

All of this is important for you to understand, because if you hold incorrect data in your heart, and you do not see yourself for who you truly are, then you will never be able to manifest everyday miracles. The truths you need to completely understand are not difficult, but getting them right makes all the difference. Truth is often too simple. We often feel, erroneously, that in order for us to do something spectacular, we need to have a Ph.D. God did not make His truth to require a Ph.D. in Divinity. When you live by these truths, you can speak without hesitation and without the fear that you won't get what you desired.

In spite of all of our power as children of God, keep in mind that Jesus told us that there will definitely be wars between nations, earthquakes, famines, plagues, and fearful sights, but that we are not to worry because all these things must come to pass and they are somehow all to God's own purpose. Jesus goes on to say, "But not even one hair of your head will perish" as a result of these events (Luke 21:11-19). Go ahead and quiet the hurricane if that is what is on your heart to do, but in the grand scheme of the tragedies going on in the world, it is but one event. You definitely do not have to stand by and watch dispassionately while your house blows away, saying "It must be God's Will." You can always know what God's Will is in any situation concerning you. God wants you to prosper and be in good health (3 John 1:2). He wants your children and their children's children to enjoy the same. He desires you to have joy, happiness, a sound mind, contentment, and live a long life (Psalms 91).

Many people tell me how they mourn for the suffering of the world. They are angry at the adversary. They worry about the state of the world. All of these demonstrate fear. When you worry, you are afraid (fearful) that things won't work out the way you want. In anger, your heart is not in an optimal state of perfect love. Anything other than perfect love is simply less, and we do not want to ever be less than we now know to be! Jesus said in John 14:27, "Peace I leave with you, my peace I give unto you: not as the world gives, give I to you. Don't let your heart be troubled, neither let your heart be afraid." How cool is that! Do you still think it is okay to worry about anything? Although He said He has given you peace, He also said YOU must not LET your heart be troubled or afraid. It is always your decision. Put on God's light! Walk in God's light at all times and all becomes available to you. (Romans 13:12)

Unfortunately, very few of us can look around and see evidence of any miracles in anyone's life. The truth and the "how to" of it all is so simple that it has eluded most of the greatest minds in every generation. If you want everyday miracles, you must choose to constantly operate with the mind of Christ, letting go of the old ways of thinking. However, most people want to take what they think is the easy path; to continue living and thinking however they want. Then when they have need or are in trouble, they call out to God to fix it or provide for them. This is not playing by God's rules, and therefore it rarely works.

The truth is that God created all the heavens and the earth. He could have made us robots, programmed to love Him. But the Word that we have now accepted as perfect and true says we must be transformed by consciously and purposefully renewing our minds to God's ways in every moment (Rom. 12:2). In computer language, this transformation means we are purposely and consciously deleting our old self and our old ways of thinking, and purposely and consciously inputting the corrective data of God's truths *and* God's light, *and* God's love. God will not and does not "possess" us, causing us to do things we don't want to do; we must exercise our free will thinking to seek God's Will, which is His Word, the Holy Bible, rightly interpreted as it was originally given.

In doing so, we are renewed in our minds, in the way we think and perceive life, and in our new awareness of our oneness with God. This is done by:

- First accepting Christ as God's way back to Him (Romans 10:9-10).
- Knowing, perceiving, or having the faith that through Christ, we now receive God's Holy Spirit, who will be our comforter, guide, and teacher, teaching us all things so that we can know all dimensions.
- Seeing the true meaning of Jesus' teachings as revealed to us by and through the Spirit (John 14:26):
    - Now are we heirs of God, and joint-heirs with Jesus (Rom. 8:17), children of God who are absolutely complete in God. (Col. 2:10) (How then can we be lacking in anything?)
    - As one is immature (a child) even though joint-heir, we must be trained in God's truth, reaching

for the highest level of spiritual achievement in God's love; only then can we fully manifest the fullness of God's power. (Gal. 4:1, Eph. 4:14-16, 1 John 4:18, Phil. 3: 15)

- Now are we part of God's one body, no longer separate from Him. (Gal. 3:28)
- God sees you as perfect, as He is perfect. (Matt. 5:48) Therefore we should see ourselves in this manner, even when we look in the mirror. Seeing ourselves as perfect should be the mental image and heart knowledge we carry of ourselves.
- God desires you to seek constant communication with Him, not through vain repetitions, or vain "good works," but through seeking Him in the silence of your spirit, and actively walking, each moment, in the Spirit and in the light of His truth and love. (Matt. 6:7)
- We may boldly go to the Father with our needs and say, "Father, you know my needs, and I thank you for their fulfillment at this present moment!" (Heb. 4:16) (Matt. 6:8)

2

HEAD KNOWLEDGE VERSUS HEART KNOWLEDGE

You will manifest signs, miracles and wonders!

How is a person going to learn to walk with all the greatness of the power of God unless he begins putting the knowledge of God's Word in his mind, meditating on it, deeply contemplating it until it becomes heart knowledge, and then living by it (Prov. 4:3-23)?

I promise you that if you will empty your mind and heart of what you used to think (renew your mind), let go of the past, live only in the moment, and fill your mind and heart with God's truth (II Tim.2:15), your prayers will be answered, and you will manifest signs, miracles and wonders (Eph. 1:17-23)!

You won't need to be anxious and hurry, battling to get through the tasks of the day. If you will trust that God is working via the Christ in you to manage all situations, you will become poised and find new efficiency in all things (1 Chronicles 29:11-12, Prov. 3:5). When faced with potential problems, you now respond and react from your heart of love. Old ways of thinking will fall away and new ways of thinking will prevail. Later in this book, you will learn that these are not simply nice words and concepts, but there is a function of the hypothalamus and the brain that God designed to enable you to consistently function with a heart of love.

When you live in this manner, you are not determining your actions from your socially-conditioned head knowledge, but from God-conditioned heart knowledge. God will make your day flow smoothly (Prov. 3:8).

To be rewarded in this way, one must only get a few key truths to move from momentary, inconsequential, and powerless head knowledge to powerful, reality-changing heart knowledge.

> *To be rewarded in this way, one must only get a few key truths to move from momentary, inconsequential, and powerless head knowledge to powerful, reality-changing heart knowledge.*

Gary Sinclair, the author of *Your Empowering Spirit*, taught me this exercise to get a feel for the difference between head knowledge and heart knowledge. Go to a mirror. Get real close. Look right into your eyes and say to yourself, "I really love myself." Say it again, but this time, listen to what your heart of hearts says. Say to yourself, "I love you," or "I like how you look," repeating these three times. When you say this, does your heart say to you, "This is truth," or does it say, "These are just words that I don't believe"? If it says it is truth without hesitation... great. Then say, "I totally like who you are," or some other statement like this. If you feel it is just words and not true, then you have just experienced what simple head knowledge is...just words and concepts. Look into your eyes in the mirror once more; say now the opposites of these statements. Can you feel the difference?

Of course this is just an exercise, but the concept can be used to determine whether anything you know is simply head knowledge or truly heart knowledge. Too often the heart knowledge believed to be true is the negative statements.

To move any thought from simple head knowledge to formative heart knowledge you must meditate. To meditate one must find absolute quietness or silence in your mind. From this silence, focus all that you are on the truths that you are having trouble owning. In this case you are not meditating with the goal of achieving "no mind," as is taught in many eastern meditation techniques, but with the goal of completely focusing upon and considering all aspects of a single

Heart knowledge is truth that you own; it shapes you; it is readily available to you without effort.

true and good thought until it goes from head knowledge to heart knowledge.

How do you know when you have successfully moved a concept to heart knowledge? You can test it by repeating the concept or thought, as we did in the mirror exercise, and listening to your heart. Does your heart say the concept is completely true?

Heart knowledge is truth that you own; it shapes you; it is readily available to you without effort. Of course, sincerity is no guarantee for truth, so you must be careful what you put in your heart.

When a thought becomes heart knowledge, it changes your body's liquid crystalline-matrix.

Every single tissue in the body is now known to be a liquid crystal. Crystalline arrangements of tissues, which we call the crystalline-matrix, are now known to be the rule instead of the exception in all forms of life. Research has determined that all living tissues, whether body tissues or microbes, are made up of unique molecular crystalline structures. These living, pliable crystalline structures are capable of creating, transmitting, and receiving laser-like bio-photons (energy packets of light, generated by the tissues of the body) for the purpose of communication between tissues and molecules.

The crystalline-matrix pathways connect every aspect of the human being to its internal and external environment. These pathways enable the body to adapt at virtually the speed of light to changes in and around the body.

This crystalline-matrix enables your body to instantly change its shape in subtle ways in order to adapt to changes in your internal and external environment. The body's ability to adapt and transmit information is clocked at less than a hundred-trillionth of a second. To put this speed into perspective, if each trillionth of a second contained the equivalent knowledge gained in one whole second, each second would represent the accumulated knowledge gained over the course of 32,000 years! Theoretically, all knowledge from all ages has been passed on to us via the light of our body that is present in the egg and the sperm.

You can think of this liquid crystalline-matrix as an intricate fiber-optic network, since it does indeed transmit the bulk of the information throughout the body via light, called biophotons. Imagine your body is constantly morphing or changing shape, literally at the speed of light, in reaction to your *thoughts* and in reaction to changes in your external environment (Romans 12:2)!

The following is a story in the Bible that demonstrates how a spiritually and physically clean person can sense his body shifting in reaction to his internal and external environment. In Luke 8:43-48, Jesus was walking with His disciples through a crowd, and a woman with an issue of blood reached out and touched the hem of His garment. She believed that in doing so she would be healed, and she was healed. Jesus stopped and said, "Someone just touched me," and the disciples said, "But of course, we are in a crowd, everyone is touching us." Jesus replied, "No, I felt *virtue* leave me." That word "virtue" is the word "dunamis" in the original Greek text. It literally means "inherent power or energy!" Jesus felt a drain on His energy.

You see, the cleaner your temple - your body, mind and spirit - the more sensitive you become to changes in your internal and external environment (1 Corinthians 3:16, 2 Corinthians 6:16). In a cruder way, you can liken this to the first time you smoke a cigarette or cigar; a clean body will immediately let you know that this is poison and send you signals like nausea and lightheadedness. Another example: after years of drinking soft drinks, you finally break the habit and haven't had any for months. The first time you try a sip of soft drink, you will be shocked at how nasty and syrupy it really tastes. In the same way, in all aspects of life we must consciously and purposely clean God's temple, which is our body, mind, and spirit. This most definitely includes cleaning up your thinking.

Every thought is every cell's command to make that thought come true! It is now believed by top researchers that our thoughts cause the mind to set up a morphogenetic field, which in turn fuels bio-holographic projections in the heart. These projections use biophotonic emissions to transmit information and control inputs to the DNA and from the DNA to the entire crystalline-matrix to support the thought command. In lay language, our thoughts send commands to the heart, which then imprints the DNA with the information to make the thought command come true.

Therefore, if we allow our selves to become depressed, every cell takes the thinking as a direct command. Every cell will become hypo-functional

> *Every thought is every cell's command to make that thought come true!*

(depressed) in order to support the thinking mode you are in. Here again we see science validating the truth of God's Word, which says, "As a man thinks in his heart, so is he" (Prov. 23:7).

Heart knowledge is held in focus and is readily available all the time, especially when compared to head knowledge, which is fleeting and flitting about from moment to moment.

God's Circle of Knowledge and Wisdom

God gave us direct insight to understand how He wants us to ultimately gain "advanced-level" knowledge. While He did direct us to meditate on His words using our mind (acquired head knowledge), He goes on in Proverbs 16:23 to reveal that once a man has gained true heart knowledge, "The heart of the wise teaches the mouth and adds understanding to the lips." Did you understand this? God's Word says this same basic thing in other places in the Bible. It is the Circle of God's Knowledge and Wisdom.

Here is how it works. You study God's universal truths, learning them through deep consideration and memorization, thereby acquiring head knowledge. You meditate, pondering

> *"The heart of the wise teaches the mouth and adds understanding to the lips."*

these truths, until they imprint the heart, making head knowledge become heart knowledge. The heart knowledge is not rote memorization any more. The heart is now wise concerning the truths you have placed there. Now full of wisdom, the heart begins to teach the mind. This brings an understanding that is greater than the accumulated knowledge gained by using our five senses. To complete this circle, you must speak it to others. We know we must open our mouths and speak it to others, because the point is that your heart is "streaming" Christ-consciousness to give you the words to say. From this "Circle of Light," one can view the world with a new sense of knowingness and wisdom beyond the five senses. This knowingness and wisdom is an *everyday miracle by God's design*!

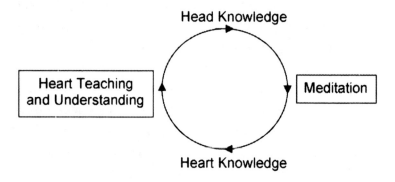

Head Knowledge

Heart Teaching and Understanding

Meditation

Heart Knowledge

I have cultivated this sixth sense of "knowingness" over the years by applying the concepts of God's Circle of Knowledge and Wisdom. From my personal experience, I can tell you that it has been only in the last few years that I began to really realize heart teaching. At first it was very sporadic. Almost every time it came, it was when I was teaching and counseling someone. I would speak and be just amazed at the words coming out of my mouth. So amazed that often I would have to stop and write it down so I wouldn't forget. It seems that the cleaner I make my body, mind, and spirit, God's temple, the more heart teaching and understanding I receive. Now, on some days, my "knowingness" is almost constant, a condition that is very beneficial as a doctor.

In a conversation with James Oschman, Ph.D., the author of *Energy Medicine, The Scientific Basis*, he revealed that the latest heart research being gleaned from around the world shows that the heart has a brain of its own. The heart knows/perceives things 5-10 seconds before the brain in your head!

Oschman writes, "Neurocardiology researcher J. Andrew Armour, M.D., first proposed that there is a functional heart-brain. Later research performed by John and Beatrice Lacey of the National Institute of Health has demonstrated that about 65% of the cells in the heart are identical to brain neurons." While researchers are not certain the connection, heart surgeons have known for years that there is a spot on the heart which, when touched, causes the patient to immediately die without hope of revival! No wonder God placed so much importance upon the heart.

I challenge you to cultivate your heart brain and to live your life as God intended, with heart knowledge!

Dr. Oschman's book mentioned above, and his latest book, *Energy Medicine in Therapeutics and Human Performance*, are a "must read" for anyone wanting a greater understanding of the science and application of energy medicine, physiology, biophysics, and the beauty of God's design. These books are easy to understand and are extremely well referenced to the scientific sources. People fear what they do not understand, and this is why most of the world will still swallow highly toxic pharmaceutical drugs, instead of opting for the more scientifically sound energy medicine that strives to restore and work *with* God's perfect design of the human body.

You may wonder at my glowing endorsement for Dr. Oschman's books. It is because there are only two modes of thinking and operating in life. You are either thinking and operating from fear or from love. If what you hold to truth in your heart is based on incomplete or inaccurate data concerning how the human being works, then it breeds fear. Fearful thinking creates chaos and what we call disease, because your thoughts sent the fear to the heart and the heart imprinted chaos into the DNA. Dr. Oschman's books reveal the beauty of God's design of the human body and its inter-actions with the universe.

Just how important is our thinking? Can it really alter matter? What does it have to do with your desire to live an *"Everyday Miracle"* kind of life? New research performed by Dr. Masaru Emoto and reported in his book *The Message in Water: Take a look at Ourselves* sheds more light on these questions. Dr. Emoto developed a technique to document the crystalline changes seen in frozen water crystals when the water is imprinted with positive or negative thinking. Water that was purposely exposed to positive thoughts, like love and thanks, when frozen, created an amazingly orderly and beautiful six-sided crystal. Water that was exposed to negative thoughts like hate and fear and then frozen created totally chaotic, dead water structures, with no resemblance to anything beautiful or crystalline. The genius of Dr. Emoto was his realization that the changes that occur in liquid water in reaction to our thoughts and prayers would be revealed only when the water was frozen.

The Bible has many references to "living water," and in the Old Testament God instructed the children of Israel that if a fly or bug fell into their glass of water, they were to throw out the water and break the glass! One might say this was because of germs, but it could also be because of the energetic shift that happens in all water, which causes it to be imprinted with the energy of anything it comes in contact with. Is water imprintable? Can it shift energetically in reaction to very small energetic impulses, such as human thought or a bug's energy? Definitely!

Now consider how true God's Word is when it tells us to resolve all conflict quickly; to love God with all your heart, mind, soul, and strength and your neighbor as yourself; to let go of the past and the ugliness therein; and to not be anxious about the future but to trust Him in all things. Especially in light of this research revealing the truth of God's Word, we develop a greater appreciation for the verse stating, "Keep your heart with all diligence, for out of it are all the issues of life" (Prov. 4:23). An expanded understanding of this verse would be, "Guard the heart as the great citadel, for out of it are the source and outgoings of life!" Because a well-hydrated human body is made up of about 80% water, the other 20% being the crystalline-matrix, what you hold in your heart truly holds the power to change your physical matter and your physical body.

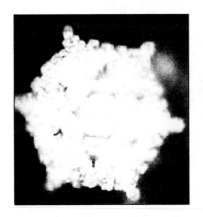

Love and Appreciation   Thank You

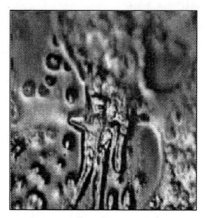

You make me sick.
I will kill you.

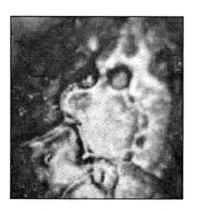

Polluted Fujiwara Dam water, Japan,
before offering a prayer

Same Fujiwara Dam water, after offering a prayer

The Law of Believing

You will manifest what you hold as truth in your heart. Therefore you will create and project that which you believe to be truth in your heart, whether negative or positive in nature (Job 3:25-26). This means if you believe life is unfair and tough, then your heart will shift the crystalline-matrix and imprint the structure of the water within your body. It will empower the DNA (which just so happens to be surrounded by six-sided, crystal-shaped, hexagonal, clustered water molecules) to create that reality (Horowitz, L.,2004, *DNA: Pirates of the Sacred Spiral*)!

If you believe in your heart that your body cannot or will not heal itself, then things will only get worse. Wrong thinking is deadly...it means that you do not love God in your heart, nor do you love yourself, nor can you love others.

Always remember that you are called to the universal truth to be the embodiment of God's love – loving God, yourself, and your neighbors as yourself. There should be no separation between us when there is love.

Wrong thinking and having the wrong heart create miracles of darkness. It takes just as much energy of living out of sync with God's love to create bad events as it takes living in correct alignment with God's way to create miracles of light and love. Pray and meditate on this and you will see its truth. You are the creator of all adverse events in your life (2 Peter 1:9, 2 Peter 2:1-2). You are so obviously responsible for operating in accordance to God's design to manifest His power in everyday miracles (2 Peter 1:2-10).

3

SUPERCHARGING YOURSELF FOR MIRACULOUS LIVING

I will see it when I believe it in my heart!

If you want to supercharge yourself for miraculous living, you must meditate on the concept of loving God until it truly becomes intimate heart knowledge. God's Word says that you must love the Lord your God with all of your heart, mind, strength and soul. We cannot love what we do not

> *We cannot love what we do not trust. We cannot have faith in what we do not believe to be true.*

trust. We cannot have faith in what we do not believe to be true. To trust means to have no fear. Fear and love are the polar opposites of the universe. If you are a worrier, you are operating in fear. If you seek to know your horoscope, you are operating in fear. If you are angry, frustrated, irritable or experiencing any other negative condition, you are operating in fear.

I hear people saying all manner of garbage: "If only my husband / wife would stop ____ my life would be great," "If only my boss would do ____," "My son or daughter hurts me so much," and "If only I could get ahead of the bills." All of these statements indicate a complete absence of love and trust in God, and absence of faith that God has only good planned for you in every situation, no matter what it looks like. "'For I know the plans I have for you,' declares the Lord, 'plans to prosper you and not to harm you, plans to give you hope and a future'" (Jer. 29:11).

It is interesting that the above negative statements also operate against what science is revealing about God's perfect design of your body. Dr. Oschman states, "A serious misconception is that what we refer to as *sensation* and *cognition*, *learning* and *memory*, and *consciousness* and *mind* are activities that reside primarily in the brain." We know that all human thoughts are extra-low frequency (ELF), electromagnetic waves. The U.S. Navy is now using radios with ELF waves to communicate with submarines far away and deep under the polar icecaps. ELF waves are not restricted by space and distance, the way a walkie-talkie signal can be blocked by a mountain or simply fade with distance. Your thoughts are being broadcast to the world! In a way, you are aiding and perpetuating the negative aspects you wish to change in other people by your negative or fearful thoughts!

In his book, *Energy Medicine in Therapeutics and Human Performance*, Dr. Oschman reports that "Research at the Institute for Heart Math (McCraty, Atkinson & Tomasino 2001; McCraty et al. 1998) has shown a relationship between emotional state and the frequency spectrum of the electrical signals from the heart. Feelings of love, caring, and compassion, or of frustration and anger, will affect the signals produced by the heart. These signals are conducted to every cell in the body *and are radiated into the space around the body"* (Emphasis added).

The heart's magnetic field has been documented to be 5000 times stronger than the brain's field, projecting out from the heart at least 15 feet and potentially infinitely.

God instructed us to seek Him first, allowing His love to flow through us, permeating the entire world, constantly! When we consciously walk in God's light and love, that light and love will be felt by all mankind and all creation, both of which will respond by peacefully and joyfully providing you all that you need. These everyday miracles are not created by the force of your own will, or by strongly concentrated thinking, but by the will and grace of God operating in and through your heart of love. You will be amazed at the everyday miracles that go on around you when you consistently operate with a heart of love.

Operating with a heart of love is not the result of a one hour "quiet time" with you and God first thing in the morning, or the last thing before bed. This is an ongoing, "every moment of every day" walk in the light of God's love - guarding your heart with all diligence, capturing every thought before it is thought to ensure it is in perfect alignment with God's love. This is not an "I've got to be intense and uptight because I have so much to do," kind of thing. This is a de-pressurization no matter the external situation; deadline or no, you trust God to never let you down. Realize your littleness, vanities, and self-delusions. Let go of the past and all worry, doubt, and fear. As you realize the true nature of God and being a child of God, you manifest Him in your life in everyday miracles. The more you will use this principle, the more you will see His power working at all times!

Please! Go ahead and test it out! The longer you properly maintain your oneness with God with no reservations, no protective walls, nothing held back…what I call being naked with God and being okay with it…cultivating a giddy love like newlyweds…the greater the rewards, and the greater the miracles! I promise you that even if you only spend one hour and a half completely aligning yourself to God's perspective of who you are in His light and love, you will see miracles just in how people treat you. However, the longer you continue in God orientation, the greater the magnitude of miracles. You will walk around as I do, in complete amazement at the smallest differences. You will be so intoxicated with the feeling of God's love indwelling you that you will seek him out diligently like an addiction. You will notice people act differently around you. They are nicer; they may give you things at times and go out of their way to help you.

Just to reiterate, we must allow God to enter the highest consciousness within ourselves. This is done by not ignoring God, but listening to His voice, and by developing your sense of "knowingness" of heart knowledge and wisdom. Learn to trust your sense of heart knowingness in all things, because at first you may think it is just your head simply being convinced of your correctness, instead of a true heart lesson.

I want to mention here that you risk losing your heart knowingness if you abuse it with people. Abusing it would be telling someone you are correct about a situation because "you have a heart knowingness from God" when actually you are consciously, or at least on some level, manipulating the situation to your favor. God's power working in and through you is not to be played with at all! It is real, and it operates on the pureness and cleanness of your heart.

Your tiny mustard seed's worth of faith (believing in things not yet seen) will grow larger as you see God work everyday miracles for you. Most people say, "I will believe it when I see it!" You must say instead, "<u>I will see it when I believe it in my heart</u>!"

Start your day by consciously magnifying your Christ-consciousness, your oneness with God. How do you magnify the Christ in you? You constantly look for opportunities to speak God-truths. Weave your work and words with God-truths in a verbal and energetic tapestry as you communicate to people in your day. When you enter a building that feels energetically thick and fear-saturated, consciously and purposely allow and project God's light and love to fill every one and everything in that space. You will be amazed at the difference and mortified over how you lived your life for so many years. Likely you were just wading through life and being a victim of your and everyone else's energetic poop!

> *Most people say, "I will believe it when I see it!" You must say instead, "I will see it when I believe it in my heart!"*

You may wonder if one person's love can overcome the fear of a thousand people. Just as there is no darkness so dark that it can blot out the tiniest spark, so too no magnitude of fear and negativity can persist as you expand God's love and light through you.

Another way to magnify God's light and love in you is to speak with God in your spirit silently during the moments of opportunity that occur as you are going throughout your day. Thank God for flowing through you His power, knowledge, wisdom, understanding, and peace.

You may also magnify God's light by intentionally increasing and projecting God's light and love from your heart zone. Feel the energy with your spirit. Visualize it engulfing other people with your spiritual eye.

You must maintain the faith (believing in things not yet seen) that God will do the work in every situation. This means you can only do what you know to do in your day, say what you know you should say with a heart of love, and leave God's part to God.

Read enlivening, energizing texts of God's truths, such as God's Word. There are many good books that are listed in the appendix. Revitalize your heart knowledge by reviewing and meditating upon universal truths of God's light and love. Feel the excitement of the day of potential miracles building in every cell of your body. Magnify God's light and love, and take time to actually feel His peacefulness and power filling you like a battery. Forcefully cause that power to radiate and fill the world around you and send its cleansing light to spiritually clean your house, workplace, and every place you go (Rom. 12:3).

You cannot be passive about any of this; be active and passionate, consciously and purposely pursuing right application of the knowledge of how your body is connected to the rest of the world and how God's love is magnified and applied for everyday miracles.

Verbally give yourself permission to radiate God's light and love to all the people you have known in the past and all that you will meet each day, knowing that every cell will accept the command and bring it into reality. Give thanks to God for everyone you have ever met, for it is the good and bad that has brought you to this moment and realization of what you desire to become as a child of God.

From this start of your day, love what you do for "a living." If you cannot love what you are doing, then what profession would you love? Move towards that profession with confidence. It may be that if the priorities in your life are rearranged, making the love-empowered and clean temple approach to life your priority will reward you far beyond the material gains of your present occupation.

Approach each day with joy and expectation, knowing you will be able to empower people through knowledge and healing. Be honored to be able to help others along in their journey.

You are separate from all the suffering of other people. The only things you are one with are your spouse and God in everyone. You are not one with other people's negativity or their emotional state. Be God-like in your Christ-consciousness so that you can view the situation as the ONE who can empower them to heal their body, mind, and spirit.

Start every day committing all that you do and say as unto Him. We are instructed in the Bible to put on the mind of Christ, to put on our armor of love and truth (Phil. 2:5, Eph. 6:11). When correctly interpreted, the word *Christ* is the Greek word *Christos*, meaning *anointed*. "Putting on the mind of Christ" here refers to the conscious and purposeful putting on of the mindset and heartset of the anointing of God's light and love upon our being. From this we can see that it is always a free will choice to live this way...you can take it off or put it on at will. You must take full responsibility for your own actions and thoughts. All day, every moment of every day, you must build love. Never fight fear! Build love! Enhance your ability to realize and maintain *perfect love*! Fighting the urge to worry, doubt, and fear is ineffective! The fighting of fear simply embeds you deeper into the fear, whatever name we call it: depression, anxiety, worry... The only protection from fear is in grounding yourself in absolute love! We know this from the Bible, "Perfect love casts out all fear" (1 John 4:18). Do you understand how important this is? You must spend all the energy you were using to "fight the fear" and use it instead to meditate on and expand your absolute trust and love. Then and only then will fear of all types disappear. Work to attain the perfection -- perfect in body, mind, and spirit. Visualize yourself as you desire to be until you breathe it into being! Acknowledge to yourself, as heart knowledge, that you are a divine being, a true Child of God. Know in your heart that He will supply all your needs, now and forever.

God said if you will but learn to trust and love Him, He will make your way perfect, *and* direct your path, *and* fill your heart with gladness, *and* establish your thoughts *and* heal all of your pain and suffering...NOW...INSTANTLY! All of this is so that you can live a "MORE THAN ABUNDANT LIFE!" If you can flip the imaginary switch in your brain and heart that would enable you to truly walk in this manner, all of this would instantly be yours to know and carry along each step of the day. Unfortunately, few of us seem to be able to really "be God's love." Most of us will need to learn over time and through diligently applying God's universal truths until we learn to be unchanged by our life circumstances (Phil. 4:11).

God told us to meditate on the truth of His Word day and night. He said this because He knew that by doing so we would be able to achieve perfection (Matt.5:48). When you meditate, you consider a thought deeply, intensely, and from all angles until you can accept it as truth in your heart and not just in your head. I suggest you start with all of the truths I told you up to this point. Take each point one at a time, and consider each until you know it to be true – not just because it comes from the Bible, but because you know it is true and that truth has changed you forever!

God said much about the value of heart knowledge. God looks at the heart more than the mind

We cannot love our neighbor if we have no love for our self.

of man. **From scientific research we now know that the mind imprints the heart, and the heart directly encodes the DNA to create the reality of the negative or positive "truths" we have sent to our heart.** This is God's perfect design being made manifest by science. God told us to "guard your heart with all diligence." God also told us to "...take all thoughts captive...." It sounds like God was telling us some important keys to living healthy, happy, drug-free lives.

We are instructed to love our neighbors as ourselves. We cannot love our neighbors if we have no love for God and ourselves. Love comes only from God, and everyone that loves is a child of God and trusts and knows God (1 John 4:7-8).

The word "love" is used too loosely in our society, i.e. "I love roller coasters," "I just love pizza," and such. God places great importance on love. It is God's love working in and through us that drives every miracle, and indeed every healthy, life-sustaining input. I see the frivolous use of the word love as a destructive force; it de-powers God in our lives when we throw the term "love" around like it is a common adjective, instead of what it truly is, a powerful verb!

As a parent, I have raised my children to know when using the word "love" is appropriate by saying, "You can only say that you love something that loves you back," so instead they say, "I really like roller coasters."

So, what exactly is love? Is it extreme like? Is it just a warm fuzzy feeling? Is it sexual attraction? From a scientific view, love creates a specific energetic frequency felt all over the body. Just as mental depression causes a specific energetic frequency and a subsequent hypo-functioning of every cell, love creates the energetic frequencies that optimize the function of all aspects of the body.

Love at its purest form is the realized love of God working in and through a person who has reached the highest level of spiritual achievement. This is called "perfect love" in the Bible (1 John 4:18). Perfect love is the point wherein all things physically, mentally, and spiritually become possible. It is at this point when everyday miracles are realized as every moment miracles!

God is Love and Light, and He abides in you. Every cell in your body is energetically charged. Romans 8:11 says,

"...He (God) will quicken (vitalize) your mortal bodies by His Spirit (light and love) that dwells in you."

God's love is brought to perfection in you when you truly love Him, yourself, and others.

When you achieve perfect love for God, yourself, and everyone else, then all things become possible. All fear, doubt, hurt, and worry disappear, because you trust your Heavenly Father to be in perfect control of all things (I Chronicles 29:11-12). You are not thinking God's cup is half empty or that He is insufficient in whatever life circumstance you find yourself. His cup is overflowing, and He has only plans for good for you.

No one can hurt you, because they feel God's love in you; you speak and show love to them repeatedly because you truly love them, thereby turning their heart from darkness.

> *Love at its purest form is the realized love of God working in and through a person who has reached the highest level of spiritual achievement.*

I was in Africa recently, in the country of Ghana. The "Abrunis" (white missionaries) who had been there for years were full of advice cautioning that if you are not careful, someone may put juju and voodoo curses upon you. They were full of advice about situations that could lead to being beaten literally to death by mobs if they think you stole something, or if you accidentally hit someone with your car, you may be raped or robbed. While it is good to walk wisely, the effect of their heart in the telling was pure fear-mongering. The younger missionaries were struggling with having been infected with fear, to the degree that they would rarely venture out of their house.

I was blessed to liberate these young people from fear by teaching them that if they truly love God, themselves, and their neighbor, as God instructed, then their path would be made smooth and perfect. In all of Jesus' travels he was never raped, robbed at sword-point, or beaten by thieves. Experiencing any of these negative events would not be the result of God "making your way perfect!" If we love God we trust Him completely. As a result of this realization, I and the missionaries were able to walk boldly and without the slightest fear through the incredible sights and sensory overloading beauty of Market Centrale in Kumasi with no feeling of separation from the Ghanaians. We were free to openly walk at all times with no fear. God's grace is the word *charis* (pronounced Karese), meaning the Divine influence of God's light and love upon your heart and its reflection in your environment. We truly experienced charis.

You will never be attacked because God's light and love go before you, making your way perfect (Psalms 16:7). When you encounter a negative exchange taking place with others, take your spiritual authority and act with love, wisdom, and spiritual power over the negative situation. Accidents are a thing of the past when you maintain your correct alignment with God's truths. He is always going ahead of you, making your way smooth. As if that were not enough, He said that there will be no problems that you will come up against. He has given His angels charge over you to take care of you, no matter where you go (Psalms 91:10-13). You are a victor over your surroundings, not a victim.

Train yourself *now* to walk in God's love. It is all so easy to talk about God's light and love and how powerful we are as God's kids...*when everything in life is relatively good!* If you wait until life situations are externally bad it will likely be too late to learn to take your authority over the situation. Train, train, train...Now! Only by walking in love, now, will we be able to remain untouched and unchanged when the storms of life rage. Instead of fighting fear by trying to pray for every foreseeable problem that may arise, focus your heart intent and love upon the entire journey. See or visualize God's love beaming out from your being to saturate your path. Walk wisely as to the ways of the world and constantly monitor your heart knowingness to move with wisdom in all situations. Monitor your heart knowingness in each moment so if you feel a shift in your energy, or a pain in your body, or fear enter in, you can immediately focus on its source and clean it with God's light and love. This is the "walking in the light" mentioned in 1 John 1:5 and Phil. 2:15.

Science is beginning to document the power of the heart and its true function as the body's primary electromagnetic generator. When we continually build and expand our ability to love, by God's design, our heart's energy and function can begin to work to alter physical and spiritual reality. Achieving higher levels of love and light is how the signs, miracles, and wonders happen through us as everyday miracles.

As you consistently manifest a heart of God's love, your physical heart will instantly imprint your body's DNA to restructure the cells, dispelling all manner of diseases of the body, mind, and spirit. This is God's Will for all who love Him, love themselves, and love everyone else. It is our willing separation from God and not loving and being one with Him that leads to disease, poverty, aging, and death. To love God perfectly is the ultimate "Anti-Aging Medicine!"

Whether birth-defected or diseased of body, we must align our imperfect bodies to our now-perfect Christ-anointing, thereby literally transforming our outward bodies by the renewing of our minds, and by changing our thinking and awareness to God-thinking and awareness. This is done by studying God's perfect Word, filling your mind and heart with knowledge and understanding, and then living and walking in this light – God's light.

Your physical body can change, becoming disease or malady-free instantly, just as surely as water is turned to wine and a few loaves and fish are multiplied to feed a multitude. Since God is all and in all

> *It is our willing separation from God and not being one with Him that leads to disease, poverty, aging, and death.*

and through all, then all becomes possible to you who will believe...now!

I want you to know that what we see as small miracles is made up of the same "God substance" as what we may perceive to be major miracles, and these are no less or more miraculous.

As Jesus Christ told us, "According to your faith, be it unto you." Recall that faith is the product of expanding your ability to love. Jesus looked to God as the source and Creator of all, and He understood the mindset that He was one with

His Father. Therefore, Jesus knew there were no limitations to what He could do. Interestingly, Jesus told us that we also would be able to do everything He did and more – that as we know in our hearts the love of Christ, which surpasses all head knowledge of love, we will be filled with all the fullness of God (Eph. 3:19). By God's power that works in and through us, He will do exceedingly abundantly above all we can ask or think, so that we will glorify God forever (Eph. 3:20). Now folks, I don't know about you, but in the past I read this in the Bible, and it didn't sink in until much later that as a child of God, I am now filled with everything that God is! I can now do all things or create anything I need through the Christ *which* strengthens me (*Christ*, the anointing of God's applied love)! God <u>didn't</u> say He would do all things *for* us. He said you and I can do all things with the strength of the Christ-light and love working in and through us! Many people read this verse as "…through Christ *who* strengthens me." This would indicate that somehow Christ Jesus is the one doing the work, which it doesn't say.

Jesus gave thanks to God for the power and substance to fill every need. God is able to make all grace (undeserved favor) abound to you, surpassing your needs, so that you can be successful in any task in life (2 Cor. 9:8). Remember I told you earlier that you will see people change around you and treat you nicely? This, and so much more, is simply grace or undeserved favor. I might add here that people walking fully immersed in fear will at times be attracted by your light and at other times be repelled. However, at all times you are as invincible as your magnification of God's light. You determine its strength! We get the concept of magnifying

God's light from a verse in the Bible says, "My soul magnifies God" (Luke 1:46). The word Grace, you may remember, in the original Greek text is "*charis*," meaning, "the divine influence of God's light and love upon your heart, and its reflection in your environment." I find it fascinating that one must have light in order for there to be a reflection. The light must reflect off of someone or something in your environment and shine back at you as a reflection of the Divine light and love from your body. This reflection is experienced by us as favor, or grace. Consciously magnify God's light and love as in Luke 1:46.

You need only to follow His example; build your temple through clean living (living, eating, thinking, healing, interacting with all God's creation in such as way as to be in harmony with preserving and maintaining God's optimal design of your body, mind, and spirit), fill your heart with the knowledge of God's truths, let your needs be known to God, believe He desires you to have it, have faith that He will perform it, and speak it into being. When I speak things into being, I always add a time modifier for when I want it to happen. I say things like, "…and as a son of God, I enable God's light and love to make it so now!"

Jesus didn't simply find someone with an abundance of wine, but He caused water to be transformed into wine (John 2:1-11). And just as Elisha didn't buy the widow more oil but caused her vessels to be filled from "God substance," so are we to see our needs, or those of the needy, filled (I Kings 17:14).

You are either operating in love or fear. This means you are consciously and purposely maintaining your oneness with God, or you are consciously and purposely separating yourself from God, as Adam and Eve did in the beginning.

You have either moved negative, fear-based untruths from head knowledge to heart knowledge, or you have filled your head with truth and thereby filled your heart with God's light and love.

I encourage you to spend your time building God's temple, which is within you. Understand that God designed us so that the body, mind and spirit would be interconnected and interdependent. If the body is poisoned by drugs, toxins, and an unclean diet and lifestyle, then the mind and spirit will be held back in their ability to fully mature. (See our website, www.every-daymiracles.info for more information on ways to optimize your body, mind, and spirit.) In the same way, if your mind is poisoned with hate and

If the body is poisoned by drugs, toxins, and an unclean diet and lifestyle, then the mind and spirit will be held back in their ability to fully mature.

fear, then the body and spirit will be poisoned as well. You are God's temple (I Corinthians 3:16). If you want to become fully mature spiritually, operating in the fullness of God, then you must strive to achieve perfect function and coherence of the body, mind, and spirit. Leave the old ways in the past. It may be best to sell your TV, since later you will see that your head and heart brains do not perceive the difference between negativity in real life or negativity simply viewed in a movie or sitcom. You will feel how poisonous most TV is when you become cleaner in your Temple. The old adage "Garbage in, Garbage out" is appropriate here. Turn from your negative habits.

Stop poisoning your body and mind with recreational or prescription drugs. Most people do recreational drugs to achieve altered states of consciousness. It may be difficult to believe, but the Christ-consciousness is more powerful and is an addiction that leads to states of being that are beyond your wildest imaginations or psychedelic trips!

Seek out and find doctors who practice only God-designed healing methods (those healing techniques that do not force the body into drug-induced illusions of health but work to restore God's perfect design and function of your body through natural, non-harmful means). I've always wanted to make a bumper sticker that says, "Just Say No to Drugs & Surgery," but the truth is that until society as a whole moves to living (and raising our children to live) in ways that are in harmony with God's design, people will continue to get into trouble that only surgery and drugs will rectify. Until accidents and war are a thing of the past, we will definitely need the heroic medicine of the ER. According to research performed by Francis Pottenger, Jr., MD, and Weston Price, DDS, it takes three generations of cats fed a perfect diet to undo the adverse effects of one generation fed a poor diet (www.price-pottenger.org). What is your diet and lifestyle doing to you, your children, and their children's children? And since the body, mind, and spirit are interconnected and interdependent, if the body is compromised for three generations, then by polluting our temple we compromise the mind and the spirit of our children and children's children. Is it any wonder that millions of children today are increasingly put on psychological drugs and are suffering from what used to be considered illnesses of old age (i.e., cancer, diabetes, rheumatism, and the list goes on)? It is the result of the last three generations that were sold the illusion of "Health through Chemistry" promoted by doctors and pharmaceutical companies.

While advances have been made in our health through chemistry, all one has to do is look around. One in every two people will get heart disease. One in every two or three people you see will get cancer.

Do you want your children to be full of God's power? You must stop being selfish, thinking only of the quick-fix, and start thinking how your actions will directly affect your offspring. Train your children now to understand why they must keep their body, mind, and spirit strong and clean.

The movies are full of "powerful" kids like Harry Potter, and Anakin Skywalker from Star Wars. While these are not the role models we want for our children, they do hold a huge appeal to today's children. The principles this book presents will be a tremendous guide to encourage the true "Force," God's force, to be strong in them. Train yourself and your children to be Masters of God's light and love.

My four children are all under the age of thirteen, and they are already more powerful in God's light and love than most adults. This did not happen by passively letting the teachers at school train them. They are powerful because they are now the third generation in my family to be raised with the knowledge of how to live in ways that optimize God's design of our body. My wife and I actively teach our children these principles in what we call our "Circle of

Light" meetings before they go to bed. It may surprise you that your children want to know how to be able to manifest God's power in and through them in everyday miracles.

The question arises: how do you cleanse your temple? One way is outlined in the Bible. Cleanse and strengthen the body, mind, and spirit through fasting, prayer, and meditation (Mark 9:29). God says that if you will fast (going without food for a period of time...from 1-40 days) to cleanse His temple (your body) with the right mindset, and a heart of love, that "...your light [interesting that He says "light," understanding the crystalline-matrix and the conduction of light through the body] will burst forth as the morning sun and your health will spring forth speedily...you will have direct communication with God, and God will guide you continually..." (Isaiah 58:8-11 expanded translation). So here we see again that optimizing yourself for greater spiritual maturity and manifesting everyday miracles is not just a spiritual path or just being a nice person, but it requires a clean and healthy body, clean and healthy mind, and a clean and healthy spirit.

Interestingly, every time Jesus spoke of how to perform large miracles, He always said, "This level of work requires much prior prayer [prayer = praying and meditating] and fasting." Most people who fast for spiritual purposes simply abstain from eating for a period of time and go about their life as usual. But this isn't what Jesus said. He said, "prayer and fasting." His example was to go up on the mountain for forty days and pray (and meditate) and fast, getting away from the distractions of life. This is a true "how-to" gem for you!

Become addicted to God's love manifested in everyday miracles. According to new research by Dr. Candice Pert, the hypothalamus located at the core of your brain releases specific neuropeptides in reaction to our thoughts, what we see, and what we experience. Further research reveals that your brain cannot tell the difference between an event that is real versus something you just watched on TV or at the movies. The same neuropeptides are released. If you fill your head with negative images, negative news, or negative anything, negativity-specific neuropeptides will be released, showering your brain with these chemicals that attach to the exact same cell receptor sites as heroin would occupy! You are literally addicted to the types of neuropeptides associated with your dominant thoughts and sensory inputs. You manifest and even seek out situations, movies, and confrontations with people in order to get your "fix" or "rush" of the neuropeptides to which you are addicted!

Just like nicotine or heroin, if you attempt to discontinue it, bam! Withdrawal symptoms hit you, and you fall prey to the temptation to do or see whatever feeds your addiction.

Guess what? God said, "If you will commit all that you think, do, or say, unto Him, then your thoughts will be established" (Prov. 16:3). I used to start my day with a prayer committing all that I will do and say that day unto Him, and then I would proceed through my day, trusting that He would guide all of my thoughts. However, it turns out that this is *not* a once-a-day prayer but an every-moment consciousness! Do you see it? God created man; He created the hypothalamus to shower the brain with special neuropeptides if you consistently think as He directs, thinking only those things that are true, right, honest, of good report, pure, admirable, praise-worthy, and lovely (Phil. 4:8). A new and powerful addiction will be created, with empowering neuropeptides showering your brain, as you continue to focus all your strength, mind, heart, and soul on loving God, yourself, and others. With this new neuropeptide addiction to your "renewed mind of God," you will do all that you can do to keep the addiction going, and your thoughts will be established for sure! It feels so good that it passes all understanding, and the peace of God will keep your heart and mind in Christ-consciousness! I guarantee it! More importantly, God guarantees it (Isaiah 26: 3, Phil. 4:7)!

When your heart knowledge is complete in the minutest of detail, in God's ways – consistently filling your heart with the correctly interpreted truths in His Word, and continu-

Everyday miracles are the direct result of God's love working in and through us and for us. God does the work.

ally growing your trust, faith, and believing in Him – nothing will be impossible to you, and God will grant you above all you can ask or think.

Above all, I want you to understand that the biggest hindrance to any everyday miracle is the thinking that any of our mortal mind power or psychic phenomenon had anything to do with it. Everyday miracles are the direct result of God's love working in and through us and for us. God does the work.

It is God's Will and design for you to manifest everyday miracles in your daily life.

I am aware that many people will read a stimulating dissertation such as this and say, "That's great, but how do I actually do it?" Believe me, the how is provided here in this little book! Go back and work the references and the text in this book until you can see the how and the how becomes formative heart knowledge, yielding everyday miracles for God's glory.

4

WALKING IN THE LIGHT

Be ye perfect even as your heavenly Father is perfect!

Our initial challenge to manifesting God's power through everyday miracles is learning exactly how to live, eat, and breathe in His light and love. In 1 John 1:7 we are instructed to "Walk in the light as He (God) is in the the light...." Here now we see one of the primary keys to manifesting our Sonship (Childship) rights to everyday miracles. The word "walk" in this verse is a verb, an action word indicating that we must do and take action and not simply "be in the light."

Walking every moment in the light and love of God is not an ambiguous way of living. It is a very specific way of handling situations.

We already discussed the importance of living in a perpetual state of love of God, ourselves, and others. Now we must learn how that love is used in real life situations.

Real life is full of *potential* distractions, interruptions, aggravations and negative challenges. Recognize now that all tension in you is fear. All of these situations are opportunities to sharpen our focus on God and learn to be unchanged in our trust that God is omniscient and omnipotent and absolutely sufficient to provide all our needs.

When Peter asked Jesus, "How often shall my brother sin against me, and I forgive him? Up to seven times?" Jesus said to him, "I do not say to you, up to seven times but up to seventy times seven" (Matt. 18:21-22). He then proceeded to continually forgive until the forgiveness was universal. When faced with hate and fear, Jesus focused his attention upon love. This is the mind that we are supposed to exemplify. "Let this mind be in you, which was also in Christ Jesus" (Phil. 2:5).

When we are faced with negative situations in our daily life, we must instantly, immediately erase the perceived hurt and our knee-jerk reaction to retaliate, and respond from our true heart of love...God's love. Colosians 4:6 tells us to respond to people with all grace. This word "Grace" in the original Greek text of the New Testament is the word "*charis*." Charis is defined as **graciousness from the divine influence (God's light and love) upon the heart, and its reflection in the life.** We see again the beauty and scientific precision of God's Word revealing the importance of the heart!

> *"Charis" means "graciousness from the divine influence upon the heart, and its reflection in the life."*

In his ground-breaking and phenomenal book, *DNA: Pirates of the Sacred Spiral*, Dr. Leonard Horowitz documents much of this divine influence found in the definition of grace. Dr. Horowitz states: "DNA plays a significant, likely Divine, role in precipitating, inspiring, and sustaining life bioacoustically and energetically. The double helix is a dual function receiver and transmitter for physical and spiritual empowerment."

Recall how we discussed earlier that the mind imprints the heart, and the heart directly encodes the DNA to create the reality of the negative or positive "truths" we have sent to our heart. Now we see, in an expanded understanding of charis, that God's divine Will influences the heart, which is reflected (via the DNA) into our lives!

When we respond with God's grace (charis) imprinted upon our heart in this way, we train ourselves not to respond from our reactive mind (head and five senses knowledge), but from our new reactive *heart knowledge* of love!

We must choose every moment to give ourselves and others truly righteous thoughts, words, and deeds in response to all inharmonious thoughts, words, and deeds. To live this way we must consciously and purposely think and respond only with those thoughts and responses which are true, honest, just, pure, lovely, of good report, and praise anything worth praising or of virtue (Phil 4:8). When we do this, we will find God's light and love grows stronger not only in us, but in other people as well. We must see that God's light and love is inherent in *all* and through *all* and can be realized by *all* when applied with understanding (Eph. 4:6).

We must meet and greet every disharmony with our harmony of rightly-used light and love. It is mathematically and scientifically verified that in the world of harmonics, true and pure vibrations create perfectly formed geometric forms in matter, even in human matter. Disharmonic vibrations create only chaos and breakdown and disrupt matter.

What are you doing when you respond with love? You are forgiving the disharmony aimed at you – instantly – in the moment it is occurring!

You are now *walking in the light* of God's love and feeling it working in and through you! Romans 13:12 calls this "… putting on the armor of God's light." And later in verse 14, it encourages us to not wish for the old ways of responding: the lust to do battle and return insult with insult and hurt with hurt. Respond with instant forgiveness by focusing on the inherent love and light of God in everyone, and as verse 11 says, "…knowing that in doing so you will grow more spiritually powerful through your Christ-consciousness than when you first believed" (Expanded translation).

Here too you see another manifestation of everyday miracles as you are transformed by the constant renewing of your heart. You are now reacting to your world through your heart knowledge instead of your head knowledge.

At times you may find others are put off by your new walk. They "lust" for a fight with you, like in the old days. They want to battle with words. They may want to wax philosophical and make predictions that your new walk won't last. Interestingly, the very next verse in Romans 14:1 addresses this problem. It says for you to not shut out those who are of "weaker faith," those who may criticize your new walk. We are not to go into critical and fruit-less discussions with them. See God's light in them. Love them despite their differences. Let their walk be between them and God. However, if someone sees your new walk and wants what you have found, then do what God's Word says in Eph. 5:2, "Walk in love, as Christ Jesus also hath loved us." In Eph. 5:8, "Now are ye light in the Christ, walk as children of light." Jesus said to us, "Now are you the lights of this world" (Matt. 5:14-16). Bring light where there is darkness. Teach others how to gain truth as heart knowledge, how to walk in the light, and how to access and manifest God's power as a joint-heir with Christ Jesus.

5

EVERYDAY MIRACLES
LIVING ONLY IN THIS MOMENT

*A quiet mind, living in the moment,
is the most powerful mind of all!*

Everyday miracles will be missed if you are living anywhere but in the moment you are in. If you are daydreaming about the past or if your head is spinning from a barrage of thoughts, songs, and make-believe conversations, the miracle of God's peace will not be yours. Recall the story we spoke of earlier. Jesus felt the energy drain out of him when the woman touched the hem of his garment (Luke 8:43-48).

When I imagine and put myself in Jesus' place, this is how my typical mind would work… I'm in a crowd, so I'm looking way ahead of myself, trying to find the best path to get where I'm going. My disciples are distracting me, saying, "Master, are you going to do that loaves and fishes thing again? That was great! And by the way, are we going to have enough chairs for the next meeting?" In my mind I'm going over my last teaching, wondering if I should have said it differently, or I'm resenting the heckler that is inevitably in every crowd. I'm thinking about my next lecture.

You see, in this scenario, I'm everywhere *except* in the moment! The woman would have touched my garment, taken my energy, and I would have simply wondered why I was so tired.

If you are not living in the moment, you cannot stay clean. In the same way, a scattered and chaotic mind is too noisy to notice any of the subtle things happening in every moment.

Although I am not saying Jesus was simply "empathic" in the above story, it is interesting to note here that there are many people in the world who are "empathic." An empath is someone who can sense what another person is feeling and can literally feel someone else's physical pain, mental state, and emotional state. They can also feel an energy drain on their body when someone touches them. I want to briefly go deeper into this topic because I believe that many more people are empathic than are aware of it. If you are one of these people, then what I am about to say will help you tremendously.

The woman would have touched my garment, taken my energy, and I would have simply wondered why I was so tired.

According to the medical research tool QEEG (Qualitative Electroencephalogram), these empaths, for an unknown reason, have very characteristic brain waves different from non-empathic people.

Obviously, every empathic person is not manifesting the highest level of spiritual maturity with their ability. It is believed that any person, after years of training, can cultivate this same ability just as a child begins learning to play a musical instrument and ultimately, with training and practice, develops a mastery that transcends their training.

There are many sensitive people in the world today who can be walking along feeling fine, and they suddenly emotionally or physically crash and know not why. They often don't realize that they picked up on someone else's pain. If no one helps these people realize how to recognize when this is happening, life for them can be an emotional and physical rollercoaster.

Being empathetic is a gift when one learns to understand and use it. It must be viewed as a gift to help others by exerting God's light and love to the situation of which they have become aware.

Many of these empathic individuals become wonderful doctors and therapists due to their ability to sense problems. According to QEEG they have heightened stimulation in the right, posterior occipital area of the brain. This may be due to cerebral allergies, toxicity, infection, or trauma to the head. The brain waves are over-stimulated in the same way in all empaths. Historically, empaths were ostracized and exorcised for demons, but now thanks to QEEG's and other research tools, we know that the Beethovens and other peculiar geniuses of the world likely have had, for whatever reason, higher stimulation and amplitude of specific brain waves that gave them their gifts.

As you, the reader, continue your journey of awakening and enlightenment through Christ-consciousness, you will see a greater range of control of your brainwaves. QEEG's reveal that the amplitude of your brain waves will increase exponentially to whatever task you point your heart and mind. As perfect love replaces fear in all aspects of your life, every perception and every ability will increase to enable everyday miracles! As Jesus told us, "The things that I do and more shall you do" (John 14:12).

A quiet mind, living in the moment, is the most powerful mind of all. When tuned to "listen" to your heart perceptions of the world, you can begin to truly know yourself and detect when the changes in your own energy are yours or someone else's.

Only a quiet mind can focus purely upon a task. All revelation and inspiration occurs most clearly when the mind is perfectly still and relaxed. You may have experienced this briefly at a time when you had been focusing your entire mind on a problem, searching for a solution without results, only to find that the solution comes to you later in the still of the night when your mind is relaxed.

> *As perfect love replaces fear in all aspects of your life, every perception and every ability will increase to enable everyday miracles!*

All things become possible when the mind is still and you are living in Christ-consciousness: in the exact moment that you are in. Most people are more comfortable living in the past, or living in the hope that life will be better somehow in the future. If you train yourself and master the concept of the first sentence in this paragraph, you will find that truly all things become possible. One of the prime benefits of living with a quiet mind and living in the moment is that true contentment follows.

Our society has trained us to be "Johnny on the spot" with a ready answer to any question, and to be a problem solver. In our down time, we are taught to have a distraction going, such as the radio or television, whether or not we are actually listening. It's "cool" to be a mover and shaker, living on the edge. Most of us, unfortunately, have also been trained in every way to never relax, especially in our minds. I'm telling you now, it will take genuine effort and direction to unlearn the habits of your mind.

So just what is a quiet mind? To find out, do this simple exercise. Choose a time and place where you will have no distractions and be in no hurry. Set a timer for one minute. Close your eyes and do not allow any thoughts to enter your mind.

How did you do? If you had no thoughts cross your mind, I applaud you. Most people performing this simple test fail miserably the first time. It just shows you how a quiet mind must be achieved through training and practice. It also shows you best what a quiet mind is by showing you what it isn't. There are many techniques used to teach you how to reach a quiet mind. They are most often referred to as meditation. Before you become uneasy with visions of mystic gurus, chants and such, know now that the concept of meditation is a directive in God's Word. He tells us to meditate on His Word night and day (1 Timothy 4:15; Isaiah 26:3; Josh. 1:8). Like everything in life, in meditation there are good ways and better ways of achieving a quiet mind. We will go over some of the better ways of meditating in a later chapter.

Is it possible to have a completely quiet mind all day long? I don't know, but the first time I personally achieved a quiet mind, it felt so good that I wanted to maintain that feeling all day. Does this mean that we should all be walking around with a totally blank mind? No, but it does mean that whatever task you put your mind to will be much more focused, and the solutions will be much clearer. You see, living only in the moment that you are in, with a quiet mind, means that all your magnificent brain power is not cluttered by static energy, created by thinking and living in many different places at the same time.

We have all been conditioned to fit the mold of society. To break this mold and find out who you truly are is another benefit of living every moment in that moment and finding new realizations through living with a quiet mind.

Remember, every thought is every cell's command to make that thought become reality. And if most of your thoughts are jumbled and cluttered with static, then what reality is being created? By changing and quieting your mind in this way you can change your reality...really!

This sounds all well and good from a conceptual point of view, you may be thinking, and you are correct to a certain extent. In order to achieve a new reality, you cannot be constantly flip-flopping back and forth between your old ways of thinking and these new ways.

The better you get at maintaining a quiet mind, living in the moment, and maintaining your alignment with God, the better the results you will get. It took your entire life to create the you of today. Remember, the poisoned body will necessarily result in a poisoned mind and spirit.

Start training your mind now with a long-term vision for a new and better you now, tomorrow, and forever. You have everything to gain by making the change. If you will live only in the moment you are in and approach it with a quiet mind, at one with your Heavenly Father, all things become possible all the time. Reach out from death and mediocrity and find life, power, and contentment.

6

CONTROLLING YOUR THINKING

Your thoughts either empower you or destroy you!

The Bible instructs us to "take every thought captive" (II Corinthians 10:5). Every word in the Bible is there because God knew it to be important. God said that we should take every thought captive, because every thought you think is either poison or fuel to your body, mind, and spirit. You can never have the power to manifest everyday miracles in your life if you are constantly "changing your mind." It is one way or the other - your thoughts either empower you or destroy you!

"Death and life are in the power of the tongue: and they that love it shall eat the fruit thereof." This is a proverb from King Solomon, one of the wisest men of all time (Prov. 12: 18, Prov 18:21). You must think before your tongue forms the words.

From scientific and clinical research, we now know that life and death are truly in the power of the tongue. Remember, every thought you think is every cell's command to make it come true. It was set up that way as part of God's design. Every cell in your body is eavesdropping on your thoughts. Every cell becomes programmed by your thinking. The programming is either temporary, as in the case of a fleeting thought, or the programming is more long-term, as in a thought that is held and perpetuated overnight and beyond. It is because of this latter case that God tells us to not let the sun set upon our wrath or negative emotions. Perpetuating that negative thought pattern overnight is all that is required to program the cells to cease to function in a healthy manner.

I think it is interesting, though, that in Matthew chapter 6, verse 27 it says, "Which of you can by taking thought even add one cubit to their stature?" Remember, it is God who does the work. It is not super-honed concentration transforming water into wine or restoring perfect health. Everyday miracles require you to follow God's "Operator's Manual."

Consider the computer I am using to write this book; I am usually happy just using the word processing program. Yet there are so many other

You must know what is available before you can put it to use.

things my computer would do, things I would want to do if I knew they were available – IF I READ THE MANUAL! You see, it is the same in life. Many people are satisfied with just picking and choosing what they want to use from God's Operating Manual, The Holy Bible, and other great inspirational texts focusing on the universal truths. But can you imagine knowing God's manual inside and out, and being able to manifest God's Will, which is to grant us "Above all we can ask or think!" You must know what is available before you can put it to use.

This means that you need to be sure that you first know God and serve Him with a perfect heart, a clean body, and with a willing mind; God knows your heart and understands all the imaginations of your thoughts. Without an intimate head and heart knowledge of God's Word, and without having a true relationship with God through Christ Jesus and lining up your thoughts under His truths, your thoughts have no power to do anything but weaken and ultimately kill you. Conversely, when you follow God's way, all things become possible, all the time.

Many stories come to mind that prove these principles to be true from patients I have seen, but one stands out, as you will see. A lady came in with a prior history of breast cancer that had metastasized to the brain. The doctors had already performed a double mastectomy (surgically removed both breasts), performed brain surgery, and exhausted chemo-therapy and radiation. The cancer had recently returned in the brain, verified by various imaging techniques, and the tumor was pressing on the cranial nerves affecting the eyes. The tumor was causing her to be severely cross-eyed and have blurry vision.

On the day she received the news that the cancer had returned, she came to my office very upset. I immediately felt inspired to pray with her, and she agreed. After finishing the prayer, which took ten or fifteen minutes, I told her to stand up. She stood up and gasped and said, "I can see! Oh my, I can see!" and as I looked at her, I could see that both of her eyes were in perfect alignment! She stood there weeping with joy in my treatment room and began to read with great emphasis out loud all of the printing on the various book covers and charts in the room to prove to herself and me that she could indeed see.

I had no idea this dramatic event would be the end result of my prayer, so I told her, "Let's go show my nurse what God has done for you!" So with three other patients in the waiting room watching and hearing of her miraculous event, she told my nurse the story, after which she finished by saying in a very poignant voice, "And my doctor was going to do surgery on me!" Immediately upon saying this, she lost her eyesight again and her eyes were again severely crossed. I was standing not far away and she, now clutching the receptionist's desk for support, said in a loud and desperate voice, "Doctor David, I can't see...help me!" It was a very dramatic and intense moment, and I did the first thing that came to mind. I came up right behind her, spoke to her softly in her ear, and told her to repeat after me as I recited what I call a "Cleaning Prayer" (See Appendix). She clutched the reception desk for support, with the other patients watching in shock. The very moment we concluded the prayer, her eyes once again were perfectly restored! Now she was so overcome by emotion that we had to lead her to another room to calm down. It was with great joy in the grace of our Heavenly Father that I turned to the next patient and said, "You're next!"

Remember the word "Grace" is the Greek word *charis,* meaning *"Graciousness from the divine influence upon the heart, and its reflection in the life."* The restoring of her vision was a definite reflection of divine influence upon her heart and mine, imprinting a new message to her DNA!

I learned many gems from this event. Primary to this discussion was the power of her own thinking; how what you think truly is the command to your cells to make it come true. When she was rejoicing in the telling of her miraculous healing, all was fine, but when she went back in her mind to the past, being in her other medical doctor's office and being told he would have to do surgery, the old fear returned and the message her thoughts were sending to the cells was, "I want you to function as you were in that other doctor's office." Her cells received the message loud and clear to instantly restore the tumor and symptoms back the way it was.

What my "Cleaning Prayer" did was to bring her thinking back into alignment with the truth of God's way, apparently removing the effect of the tumor immediately. Another lesson learned was how we are to live in the moment we are in and never revisit the past to rekindle all of the emotions and fear it holds.

During every subsequent visit, this lady would return with the original symptoms back again, and every visit we would pray. Every single time she would leave with perfect vision and eyes in perfect alignment. Try as I may, I could not teach her to maintain her healing because she refused to change her thinking. Her heart knowledge was based upon incorrect data: that she deserved to die.

She wore an eye patch to help her see when she drove, due to her severely crossed eyes. On each visit she would arrive unable to see, and after I would exert my spiritual authority, enabling God to work through me, she would have perfect alignment of her eyes and perfect vision. This was from no medicine and no treatment. Each time she would prepare to leave the clinic, she would put the patch back on. I'd tell her not to use it, and she would say, "But I need it to drive." I would reply, "But you can see now." Regardless, she would return for her next visit wearing it and severely cross-eyed.

She died several months later, leaving me to wonder at why God would allow this when He so obviously could and would restore her. So I asked God, and He told me that He had honored my believing and had used this to teach me many truths that I would be able to pass on to you here.

You cannot know what and how to think correctly without knowing God and His will, which is the Word of God. You must then move this head knowledge of the Word to formative heart knowledge through meditating on His truths. However, once you know God, and His Word is in your mind and heart, and your mind and heart agree, then you must choose through your free will thinking to maintain the correct orientation of

> *You cannot know what and how to think correctly without knowing God and His will, which is the Word of God, the Bible.*

truth and reality in each and every moment, even in the face of overwhelming circumstances. God said, "If you abide in me and my words abide in you, you can ask what you will and it will be done. By this is our Father glorified, that you bear much fruit"…everyday miracles (John 15:7)! You will see it when you believe it in your heart!

7

WHO ARE YOU ON THE INSIDE?

"You are the apple of my eye"- God
Zech. 2:8

O ut of the mouth come the issues of the heart. Nothing can come out of your mouth without first being a thought. Thoughts come from the heart.

In your heart of hearts, who are you? Do you see yourself as a victim? Has your illness become your identity? Do you feel that you are a victim of genetics and inheritance? Are you who you let everyone else see? Is life just unfair? Do you feel that you are living a lie? Are you happy? Are you angry? Are you content?

Who you are on the inside, in your heart of hearts, makes all the difference in the world. All of the retraining of your mind to be quiet and live in the moment will enable you to reach new heights, but the you on the inside must line up, not with your past, and not with who you hope to be someday, but to who and what the Word of God says you are NOW and every moment. There can be no deceiving yourself.

Because it is so important, I keep reminding you that every thought is every cell's command to make it reality – to make that thought come true. This means that your body will do everything it can to support the view you have of yourself.

Consider that you never see someone who is depressed acting hyper. Their body is sluggish and they have no desire to do anything. By their free will choice to be depressed, they are sending the signal to all of their cells to not produce as many neurotransmitters, less brain chemicals, and less hormones – after all, they won't be needing them since they are not wanting to be alert, stimulated, or actively living.

I hear patients tell me how relieved they were to find out that their other doctor finally figured out that their brain was not producing enough of this or that brain chemical required for them to not be depressed. Of course there is a deficiency of the brain chemicals! The cells responsible for producing that brain chemical received your thought signal to produce less of it so that you can be depressed!

Depression can be caused by the accumulation of chemical toxins from medicines and the environment. This toxin-induced depression goes back to our discussion in Chapter 3 about keeping God's temple, your body, clean by living and healing His way (1 Corinthians 3:16, 2 Corinthians 6:16).

You cannot get stuck in feeling justified being depressed or upset or any of the other negative, poisonous emotions.

In the same manner, there are those who have been told by a doctor that they only have a certain number of days or months to live because of a terminal illness, say, six months. Of course, they die in six months as predicted. They accepted the doctor's prediction as truth and the body created the reality. There are those people who live well beyond the predictions. The people who live the longest are those who refuse to accept the prediction as their reality. Please do not place the responsibility for your illness and health on external sources.

We all physically manifest our heart of hearts. We must realize that our own thoughts and actions are an integral part of all conflict and illness. As the Word says, out of the mouth come the issues of the heart, and out of the heart comes the issues of life and death (Matt. 12:34; Matt. 15:18-19). In the book of Hosea, it also says that "We are destroyed for a lack of knowledge." Knowledge of what? Truth. What is the source of truth? God's Word and the universal truths He gave to all to know, over the course of time, through the Circle of God's Knowledge and Wisdom. Of course, you can gain in knowledge by reading or hearing. Reading and hearing puts knowledge in your mind. Meditation gets knowledge from your mind into your heart. That is why God instructed us to "meditate on my Word day and night" (Joshua 1:8).

> "We are destroyed for a lack of knowledge."

To meditate is to focus all that you are to one task until it becomes part of you. The goal is to have agreement in your mind and heart. You can see why it becomes so very important *what* you put in your mind and ultimately into your heart.

If you put in erroneous information, that will create an unfavorable outcome in your mind, body, and spirit. In this scenario, the only "everyday miracle" you will see is the sheer fact that you somehow survived the day!

If you are sick, your illness can be a blessing! It is a signpost that can lead you on a journey and down a path that needs to be followed in order to find greater spiritual maturity. Through spiritual awakening, your outward journey is taken inward and upward. With the illness as your guide, you can correct the imbalances in your body, mind, and spirit, resulting in contentment and a long, healthy life.

All meditative techniques share a common goal: to help you achieve a quiet mind. It should be clear to you that you will have a difficult time keeping a quiet mind with kids running around the house screaming and playing. Meditation techniques began just that simply. Someone determined that it was easier to meditate in a quiet, aesthetically pleasing, comfortable environment, and so on.

Knowledge of God's Word, prayer, and meditation are the foundation of a spiritual life. Prayer is the transmitter while meditation is the receiver; therefore, prayer and meditation are part of the same process. From this perspective both can be practiced anywhere and anytime. Imagine all things, complete healing included, truly being possible all the time through God-designed clean living.

> *If you are sick, your illness can be a blessing! It is a signpost that can lead you on a journey and down a path that needs to be followed in order to find greater spiritual maturity.*

8

BE ON A JOURNEY TO SOMEWHERE

Press on toward the highest level of perfection!

I often hear people say statements that seem to be universally accepted. "Life is a great journey." "It's just part of my journey." "He/she is just taking a different path." There was always something bothersome to me about these statements, but only relatively recently could I put it into words. Life is a journey where few seem to

> *Life is a journey where few seem to know their destination.*

know their destination. Few people set out for grocery shopping without knowing where they are going. Yet most of us recognize that we are on a grand life journey with no clear destination or goal. Sure, you may have goals in your career or lifestyle that you have set for yourself, but they are truly only mileposts you have established along the way to somewhere.

Now that you have read the "how" of manifesting everyday miracles and you know how to stop being a victim of circumstance, I want to give you an awareness of your ultimate destination!

Performing everyday miracles is just *part* of your journey. Healing the sick and teaching God's universal truths so that others can stop being victims is also just part of the beauty of the journey. These are not the destination!

There is an interesting story in the book of Mark, chapter 9. I bring this story up because it reveals that definitely all that we see is not all that is there! It also reveals our ultimate destination. In this story, Jesus took three of his disciples up on a high mountain away from everyone. As the disciples watched, Jesus was transfigured right in front of them. The word "transfigured" is an interesting word. In the original Greek text it is the word "*metamorphoo*," meaning to change or transform. This is where we get our terms "metamorphosis" and "morph." In the story, Jesus' clothes turned whiter than any bleach could make them, the dust and dirt of the journey fell from his clothes, and he and his clothing began to shine. As the three disciples watched, two men suddenly appeared in their transfigured form. Jesus then went over to the two men and started talking with them. The two men were Elijah and Moses, who both just appeared out of a different dimension. It does not say what Jesus, Elijah, and Moses talked about, (Luke says it was about Jesus' coming departure) but the disciples were beside themselves with excitement. Keep in mind, both Elijah and Moses lived over a thousand years prior to Jesus' birth, and yet here they were just meeting across time, space, and distance! What dimension did Elijah and Moses come from? Obviously they were not dead, nor did the Bible say that they were ghosts or spirits. The original texts indicate that they were physically there, and then when they finished their conversation with Jesus they went back to the dimension they came from.

There is no reason to think Moses, Elijah, and others who achieved spiritual perfection in Christ-consciousness, are not still around today and able to come and go at will!

It is a radical idea, but one of the first verses children learn is John 3:16, "For God so loved the world that He gave His only begotten Son, that whosoever believeth in Him shall not perish [die] but have everlasting life." It is interesting; verse 15 says almost the identical thing. It is like God wanted to be sure we really hear this and understand this statement, so He said it twice, back to back. (Also found in John 11:26.) I was always taught that our physical bodies die and then the "dead in Christ" (those who died with a Christ-consciousness – review Chapter one – that Jesus was the son of God, and that God raised him from the dead) will arise in the end times to enjoy the everlasting life (I Thess. 4:16-17). This is true; however, I believe that this inter-dimensional exchange indicates that there is so much more available. The "dead in Christ" are those people who physically died and in their life knew God but never achieved the highest level of spiritual maturity. As in all things, we all can only go as far as we have been taught.

I believe that when God revealed "you will not die," He meant you will *never* die – if you reach the perfection of your spiritual maturity. Think about it; even the "children of darkness" have everlasting life, but they are forever separated from God.

Since God says He is no respecter of persons, what is available for one is available for all (Acts 10:34). So when we see Moses and Elijah talking with Jesus over a thousand years after their time, the ability to transfigure our earthly

97

body, and the ability to not physically die, and to continue to exist in a higher dimension must be available to all. In Romans 12:2, we are instructed not to be conformed to this three-dimensional world, but to be transformed (metamorphoo) by the renewing of our minds.

If this isn't convincing enough, consider Enoch, a man spoken of in Hebrews 11:5, "By faith Enoch was translated (Translated is the Greek word Methistemi, meaning transfer, carry away, or transport) so that he should not see death; and was not found, because God had translated him: for before his translation he had this testimony, that he pleased God." Again we see that Enoch's physical body was not found. He didn't die and get placed in a coffin. In science fiction terms, he got transported to another dimension! Other verses that use the word "translate" are in Col. 1:13, "Who has delivered us from the power of darkness, and has translated us into the kingdom of His dear son," and in 1 Cor. 13:2 "...and though I have all faith so that I could remove [the words "could remove" are the same as "translate"] mountains, and have not charity [charity=agape=perfect love] I am nothing." I really like this last verse, since it reveals the reality that anyone can potentially perform miraculous feats, without having achieved the highest level of love, yet the feats will be empty of self-actualization. This explains how people without love can and do manifest miracles on the physical plane. We are called to a higher realization, that only in achieving perfect love will we find ourselves translated because we too are "pleasing to God" as was Enoch.

This knowledge is paramount to your journey since it is difficult to strive on if you are unclear as to your ultimate destination! To achieve this level of spiritual maturity, now, is your destination! Now you know where you are going. Seek translation today! It is not just a random journey through life. You are now called to take a journey through everlasting life by maximizing your temple (your physical body, mind, and spirit), bringing yourself into maximum consciousness, God's love.

Doing what is necessary to manifest God's power through you in everyday miracles is just the starting point for the unlimited potential we have as heirs to all that God is, and joint-heirs with Christ Jesus! (Rom. 8:16-17) You also may be able to meet with Moses, Elijah, and others who reached this level of spiritual maturity in Christ-consciousness.

Some may say that I am putting us on the same level as Jesus, or that He was Divine and therefore only He could do these things. However, Jesus continually pointed to the Father as the source of His words, signs, and miracles, and affirmed that the same power that works in Him works also in you (John 14:10-14). He came to teach us the ways of our Father, God, so that we may all know every dimension and be filled with all the fullness of God's power (Eph. 3:18). This power is able to do above and beyond all we can ask or think so that you will glorify Him! If that were not enough, He goes on to say that this power would be for all ages, world without end! (Eph. 3:19-21) Now I don't know about you, but I can ask and think a whole lot of things. He says that God's power, working in us, is able to do even beyond my ability to think!

In regard to the possible accusation that we are putting ourselves on the level of Jesus Christ, the Holy Bible tells us that as children of God, we are <u>now</u> joint-heirs with Christ. I am not claiming, nor have I met anyone claiming, to have the level of enlightenment that the Master has. To be a joint-heir means that we have the possibility of the same power, the same strength, and the same degree of understanding. Being joint-heirs does not mean that one has more than the other, nor does it mean that the oldest heir gets half and the others divide what is left. We now see the truth that Jesus proclaimed to us, that we would be able to do the signs, miracles, wonders, and more than He did (John 14:12).

Jesus said in Matthew 5:48, "Be ye perfect, as God is perfect." This word "perfect" in the original text is the Greek word "*teleios*," which, much like the word *teleioteta* mentioned in the preface of this book, means to be

> *To be a joint-heir means that we have the possibility of the same power, the same strength, and the same degree of understanding.*

finished, fully mature in the body, mind and spirit. This speaks to any dogma that says only Jesus could be perfect. Jesus would never have advised or expected the impossible for man. Therefore, when He told us to be perfect, He knew it was possible for all of us! The apostle Paul even admitted that he had not yet reached the full spiritual maturity that he knew to be available, but that he continued to strive toward that level of perfection (Phil. 3:12-16). Some may feel this is impossible to achieve, but your only focus in life must be the building and expanding of your ability to love. Many people get bogged down in religious dogma and theologies that do not matter. God never intended His children to need a Ph.D. in Theology to reach their highest spiritual perfection! BE LOVE! Know what God made available to you, and use it! It is just that simple.

Every issue in life is a chance to perfect your love. Every moment is a learning situation to refine your love and oneness with God. Let go of the past. The past is defined as every moment before this one. If you at first fail, correct it in love and move on. Be here, now, and live only in the moment you are in.

9

MEDIATION TECHNIQUES

Be still and know that I am God!
(Psalms 46:10)

Y ou have spent your entire life training your brain to be busy. Now train it to be quiet. The results will amaze you. Meditation and prayer can be done anywhere, anytime. In the same way that you can't go to the gym and workout a few times and be physically fit, so it is with meditation. The more you practice, the better you become and the greater the results. The ultimate goal is to train your mind to be quiet, content, and focused no matter where you are or what the circumstance.

Romans 12:2 says we are to be transformed by the renewing of our minds. This word "transformed" is the same word as "transfigured" in the Greek (Mark 9). But how do we renew our minds so that we also transfigure? One way is to get our brains in the correct gear using Binaural Technologies, which are audio CDs of frequencies that stimulate the mind to a balanced state – the left and right hemispheres of the brain are equally active and focused, or synchronized. These CDs enable you to achieve frequencies of brain waves that would take years of training to achieve, and then years of practice to cultivate. In a nutshell, all of the following meditation techniques can be enhanced with CD technology. These CDs will be available soon through our website, www.everydaymiracles.info.

Remember, if the mind is full of static energy, jumbled thoughts, and songs, then the body will do all it can to support the state of mind you are in. By quieting your mind you enable the body to heal.

It can help to meditate with someone who is more spiritually mature. They should be spiritually clean. You may want to start your meditation with a "Cleaning prayer" for you and whoever you are meditating with. Meditating with a more mature and energetic person enables you to somewhat entrain to their vibrations. If however, you feel intimidated or distracted by meditating with someone else, then let them know, in love, and find what works best for you. Meditating is your time to be your closest with God as possible.

You may also want to control your space by diffusing essential oils into the air or applying them on your skin. Frankincense, sandalwood, balsam fir oil, and many other essential oils have been used in this way in temples for thousands of years. Controlling your meditation space can be difficult when children, television, and other noises and distractions are present. You may want to invest in some headphones that block out ambient noise. There are many good gentle, nature music CD's and meditation CD's available that can help you achieve peace and clarity of heart and mind.

To enhance your meditation you may want to fast (eating nothing and drinking only water) on days that you have the opportunity to meditate for long periods of time. Often it is tempting to fast on workdays, however, the greatest effect will be noticed when all you do on these days is prayer, fasting and meditation. Remember, on several occasions Jesus told the disciples that the reason he could do more signs, miracles, and wonders was because He had done much more "prayer and fasting" than all of the twelve disciples put together! Do you want greater miracles? Do you want it badly enough to spend days and weeks dedicated to prayer, fasting, and meditating on truth and love? The more time you spend, and the greater the heart-quality of your prayer and meditation each day, the greater your ability to love will become, and the easier it will be for you to manifest true everyday miracles.

There are many different techniques. The following are a few meditation techniques to get you started.

Meditating on God's Word

We are directed to meditate on God's Word both day and night. From our previous discussions, you will recall that the hypothalamus releases neuropeptides that are specific to the type of thoughts you are thinking. By meditating upon God's truths for a prolonged period of time, as He said, "both day and night," you can see that a very specific type of neuropeptide will shower the brain, causing a chemical addiction to God and His words and His will in your life...leading to a very cool life, full of everyday miracles.

In this type of meditation, it is best to have already developed the ability to achieve a quiet mind through practicing the other methods outlined.

Select one verse from the Holy Bible that you need to get from your head knowledge into your heart. Start by looking up reference verses in this book. Focus your quiet mind upon the verse. Observe inwardly your heart. What does it say in regard to the verse? It may surprise you that your heart says that it is 'just words' and that it 'is not really true.' Conversely, it may ring true in your heart. Either way, with high intent and focus, contemplate the truth that is the verse without straying into side thoughts. Maintain the meditative quiet mind while repeating the verse. Avoid the feeling that you already know all there is to know about the verse. The goal is that your heart of hearts will accept the verse as absolute truth. At that point, the power of the Word of God is made manifest in you. Nothing, no meditation or power, is more healing than God's Word.

If you have difficulty getting a verse or concept to become heart knowledge, break it into smaller, simpler concepts or pieces. Consider each piece from all angles, and then reassemble the verse and consider the whole again. Another tactic might be to realize that a fundamental truth is needed first before the truth you are having difficulty with can be fully understood.

Also, it should be a literal "no brainer" that you can ask God for wisdom and perception, claim it as done, speak it into being and thank Him that it is done...then listen. Don't get caught up in the idea that every verse or concept can be converted into heart knowledge in one day. Stay faithful, and pursue knowledge diligently (Prov. 2:3-6).

Relaxation Meditation

Relaxation meditation is one of the most fundamental techniques. It is the starting point for many of the other types of meditation which go on to more specific goals. This technique has been shown to activate the parasympathetic nervous system and create calming alpha brain waves. Tension and pain will be released through this healing meditation.

Lay or sit with your back straight, and completely tense every muscle in your body for five seconds, unless tension will cause pain. In that case, skip the tensing step. Take three deep breaths, breathing in through your nose and out through your mouth, letting the air exhale naturally. Close your eyes. Now breathe normally, but deeply exhale while you mentally concentrate on releasing the tension. Concentrate on relaxing all of the muscles in your face, head, and neck. Now as you breathe, consciously relax in the following order: your arms, chest, abdomen, legs, feet, and toes. Finally, relax from the base of your spine, working up to the top of your head. Relax each part individually, as opposed to attempting to simply relax your entire body all at once.

Now with every muscle relaxed, continue to breathe in the same manner for 10-15 more minutes. Block out all negative thoughts and maintain a quiet mind. Focus your mind on the space between inhalation and exhalation and at the base of the heart.

Breath Meditation

This is a very simple and powerful meditation. In Breath Meditation, you lay or sit with your back straight. You should breathe normally but focus your mind on the breath itself. Feel it enter your nose and pass into your lungs. Simply watch your breathing. Breathe the air all the way into your belly for a count of eight. Relax your abdominal muscles, while holding the inspiration of air for a count of four. Exhale naturally and gently for an eight count, allowing the air to ruffle the top of the soft palate at the back of the roof of your mouth. Upon exhalation, hold your breath for a four count. Repeat and do this for twenty minutes or more. Block out all thought. The goal is to feel no separation between you and your breathing. Feel the air filling your stomach and gradually move the sensation down your legs to your feet. It will begin to feel like you and your breathing are one. Observe every stage of breathing: the inhalation, the space between breaths, and the exhalation. Pay particular attention to the space between breaths. This space is very healing.

Meditating in Nature

Meditating in nature can be very healing. If you live in a city, there are still options that will allow you to get closer to nature. Botanical gardens and some zoos, as well as city parks, can suffice. To get out away from the sounds and smells of the city is most desirable. Find a spot where you don't have to be observed or distracted.

10

MEDITATION THOUGHTS FOR EVERYDAY MIRACLES

*Seek knowledge diligently and above all
seek understanding!*

hallenge yourself with these thoughts to see if they are
simply head knowledge, just words generally accepted
as true. If they are heart knowledge each time you repeat the
thought, your heart says it is completely true and your head
and heart are in agreement. Scripture verses are provided so
that you can double up on the same concept. The scriptures
of the Holy Bible are said to be "living energy," "quick and
powerful," and medicine to all your flesh (Hebrews 4:12).
There are many truths in this book that are not listed below.
Go back through the book and make your own list of truths
that you need to move to heart-knowledge.

1. Everyday miracles are available for you. (1 John
   3:1)
2. You control your own reality. (Prov. 23:7)
3. God created us in His image to be one with Him.
   (Gen 1:27)
4. Mankind separated himself from God in the Garden
   of Eden. (Gen. 3:17)

5. God sent Jesus to give us a way back to being one with God. (John 14:23; John 1:12-13)

6. Jesus taught us that God's Will is that we live a more than abundant life. (John 10:10)

7. Everything Jesus did and more is available to us. (John 14:12)

8. Now we are heirs of God, and joint-heirs with Christ, children of God. (Rom. 8:16-17)

9. Now are we part of God's one body, no longer separate from Him. (John 17:23)

10. God sees you as perfect, as He is perfect. (Heb. 10:14)

11. God desires you to seek constant communication with Him, not through heartless mantras or vain "good works," but through seeking Him in spirit and in truth. (I Thes. 5:17)

12. If you will acknowledge God in all that you do and say, He will establish your thoughts and make your day run smoothly, and in doing so it will be as medicine for your body, and liniment to your joints. (Col. 3:17; Prov. 3:8)

13. You must convert God's truths from simply memorized data in your mind to move to heart knowledge. (Prov. 23:7)

14. Heart knowledge is truth that you own; it shapes you; it is readily available to you without effort. (Prov. 22:17b-18)

15. Believing = Receiving, whether it is negative or positive believing. (Heb. 11:1)

16. You will create and project that which you believe to be truth in your heart, whether negative or positive in nature. (Rom. 14:14b; Prov 4:23, Prov.23:7)

17. We must love the Lord our God with all of our heart, mind, and soul. We cannot love what we do not trust. We cannot have faith in what we do not believe to be true. (Mic. 6:8)

18. All thoughts of worry, doubt, and fear indicate a lessening of our love for God; a lack of real trust and faith in Him. (1 John 4:18, Prov. 1:24-33)

19. Seek God first and in every moment, by making Him your primary determining factor in all situations in your day. (Isa. 55:6)

20. Allow God's love to flow through you to the world around you! (Rom. 12:3)

21. All pressure begins in your head...consciously depressurize by trusting God in all situations. (Isa. 30:15)

22. Recognize that there is nothing powerful in and of ourselves, but that our power and authority is from our correctly applied consciousness of God's love. (Rom. 12:3)

23. The longer you maintain your "mind of Christ," the greater your love, faith, and trust will grow, and the greater the miracles you will do and see. (Eph. 1:19)

24. Your tiny mustard seed's worth of faith (believing in things not yet seen) will grow larger as you see God work everyday miracles for you. (Luke 1:37)

25. All day, every moment of every day, you must visualize yourself as He sees you, perfect in body, mind, and spirit. (Col. 1:22)

26. Know in your heart that He will supply all your needs, now and forever. (Phil. 4:19)

27. God told us to meditate on the truth of His Word, day and night. (Jos. 1:8)

28. God looks at the heart more than the mind of man. (1 Sam. 16:7)

29. The mind imprints the heart, and the heart directly encodes the DNA to create the reality, physically, mentally, emotionally and spiritually, based upon the negative or positive "truths" we have sent to our heart. (Prov. 23:7)

30. God told us to "guard your heart with all diligence" (Prov. 4:23) God also told us to "take all thoughts captive" – control your thinking. (2 Cor.10:5)

31. We are instructed to love our neighbor as our selves. <u>We cannot love our neighbor if we have no love for our selves</u>. We cannot know love if we don't accept, trust, and love God. (Matt. 23:37; Prov. 3:5)

32. God's love is brought to perfection in us when we truly love Him, our self, and others. (1 John 4:18)

33. God's cup is overflowing and He has only plans for good for you. (Amos 5:14; Jer. 29:11)

34. It is our willing separation from God in our mind, heart, and spirit that leads to disease, poverty, aging and death. (Hosea 4:6)

35. What we may see as small miracles are made up of the same God substance as what we may perceive to

be major miracles and are no less or more miraculous. (1 Chron. 29:11-12)

36. Jesus told us that we also would be able to do everything He did and more. As we know in our heart the love of Christ for the Father, which surpasses all head knowledge of love, we will be filled <u>with all the fullness of God</u>. (Eph. 3:16-19)

37. As a child of God, I am now filled with everything that God is! I can now do all things or create anything I need, through the Christ (God's anointing within us) which (not who) strengthens me! (Phil. 4:13)

38. God is able to make all grace, which is undeserved favor, abound to you, meaning surpassing your needs, so that you can be successful in any task in life. (2 Cor. 9:8)

39. Let your needs be known to God. Believe He desires you to have it. Have faith that He will perform it, and you speak it into being. (Psalms 37:5, Phil 4:6)

40. Spend your time building God's Temple which is within you. (1 Corinthians. 3:16-17, 1 Cor. 6:12-13, 19-20, 2 Cor. 6:16).

41. When your heart knowledge is complete in the minutest of detail, in God's ways, through filling your heart with the correctly interpreted truths in His Word, and continually growing your trust, faith, and believing in Him, nothing will be impossible to you, and God will grant you above all you can ask or think. (Eph. 3:20, Matt. 6:33)

42. The biggest hindrance to any everyday miracle is the thinking that any of our mortal mind power or

psychic phenomenon had anything to do with it, instead of it being from the correctly applied light and love of God. (Phil. 4:13; John 5:19, 30; Matt. 5:36, Matt. 6:27)

43. Everyday miracles are the direct result of God's love working in and through us and for us. God does the work. (John 3:21, Phil 4:19, 2 Cor. 9:8, Psalms 37:5)

I pray that God will bless you with all understanding and wisdom in the truth of His love and light. I pray that the eyes of your understanding be enlightened in the truth of His Word. I pray that you too may know the exceeding greatness of His power through everyday miracles in every moment of your life.

David A. Jernigan

Appendix 1

Please do not get caught in the mindset that any prayer is like magic words. The words do not matter as much as the realities of the truths you hold in your heart driving the intent of the words. Feel the energy of God's light and love working in and through your heart. Consciously and purposely direct your prayers downward from your mind to your heart. See the energy of your prayer beaming out from your heart like a beautiful ray of light. You can also direct the energy of God's love through your prayer down through your hands. Often people experience a very warm sensation in their hands when praying in this manner.

If you feel that your prayers are ineffectual, then in your heart you are likely asking God to do something that He said you have the power to do. Speak from a position of authority as a child of God. Remember that Jesus said even the disciples couldn't do some of the signs, miracles, and wonders that He did, because they hadn't cultivated their heart-knowingness through much prayer, meditation, and fasting. In this case, you should pray, meditate, and fast while focusing upon who you really are as a child of God and what rights this gives you. Build your ability to know love and your ability to be love. Also go back and re-read this book until you understand more fully, how to walk in power.

Do not give up! Continue in the mindset that you are invincible by design and continually work to build and expand your ability to know love of God, yourself, and others.

CLEANING PRAYER

"*I acknowledge God as the source of all power through His light and love. I now magnify His light and love and clean my vessel and this _____ (situation, person, place, or thing) and make it sacred and pure and I make it so now through the Christ that works in and through me as a child of God, for God's glory!*"

SUPERCHARGING PRAYER

"*I consciously and purposely amalgamate (blend or meld together) all that is me with all that is God. I now thank you God for empowering all that I am with your light and love. I now erase all worry, doubt, and fear by my willing trust in you, God, in all situations. I love you. I magnify your light and love through my entire being. I thank you and enable you and open myself to your love to flow in and through me in this and every day. I love myself and acknowledge that I am made perfect through your love. I love everyone else as you have made them perfect through your love. Enable me,*

I ask, to greet all I meet with love, instantly forgiving them any offense as you instantly forgive me. Through the Christ in me, Amen."

APPENDIX 2

RECOMMENDED READING

- *The Rest of the Gospel*, Dan Stone and Greg Smith, One Press, Richardson, Texas, 800-915-8771 or www.restofthe gospel.com.

- *The Life and Teaching of the Masters of the Far East*, Volumes 1-3, Baird Spalding.

- *The Message in Water: Take a look at Ourselves*, Dr. Masaru Emoto, www.masaru-emoto.net.

- *DNA: Pirates of the Sacred Spiral*, Dr. Leonard Horowitz, www.tetrahedron.org.

- *Energy Medicine; The Scientific Basis*, James Oschman, Ph.D.

- *Learning the Bible in 24 Hours*, Chuck and Nancy Missler, 800-KHOUSE, or www.khouse.org.

- *The Rainbow and the Worm*, 2nd ed., Mae Wan Ho, Ph.D., World Scientific Publishing.

APPENDIX 3

FAVORITE BIBLICAL REFERENCE MATERIALS

- *The Companion Bible,* (King James Version) The Authorized Version of 1611, Kregel Publications

- *Keyword Study Bible,* Revised 1991, AMG Publishers, Chattanooga, Tennessee

- Strong's Concordance

- *Critical Greek Lexicon*

- *www.biblegateway.com,* an internet concordance.

OTHER BOOKS BY DAVID A. JERNIGAN

- ***Beating Lyme Disease; Using Alternative Medicine and God-Designed Living***
Drs. David and Sara Jernigan, 2004

    Beating Lyme Disease is written not to simply provide the obvious facts concerning Lyme disease, but to also provide possible solutions for maximizing the integrity of the body, mind, and spirit. Drs. Jernigan wrote this book in such a way that potentially difficult concepts are easy to understand, knowing that people with chronic Lyme disease may have more difficulty understanding what they read.

    This book will help guide you to a greater understanding of what it takes to reclaim the quality of life you seek...through the latest advances in science and quantum physics, and the power of restoration available through God's light and love!

- ***Stem Cells of Light***
(To be released 2006)

    Take a scientific journey of discovery to what will likely be new realizations of the regenerative power of light. Discover how your body works via light coursing through the liquid crystalline-matrix that makes up your tissues.

The promise of regeneration; the repairing of tissue; the restoration of what has been damaged are the attraction of stem cells. It is indeed the "Holy Grail" of medicine, the unspoken implication being that we would never grow old and we would never die. Dr. Jernigan reveals how the present and future holds the purest promise of all of these hopes and dreams – in stem cells made of light.

• *Infectious Perceptions; Living and Healing in a World of Designer Microbes*
(To be released 2006-2007)

This book dismantles the "Germ-theory" which has so infectiously contaminated the minds of most of the world. How you perceive illness from microbes will radically change after reading this book. This is a real "How-to book" with specific instructions and possible natural remedies and therapies for Dr. Mom and Healthcare Professionals, dealing with everything from sinusitis to genetically engineered, designer microbes.

ONLINE RESOURCES AVAILABLE TO YOU FROM DR. DAVID A. JERNIGAN

- www.everydaymiracles.info – This is a companion site to the book, *Everyday Miracles by God's Design*, providing you with ongoing help in manifesting everyday miracles. You will find more meditation "Thoughts for Heart Knowledge" and read uplifting testimonials from others experiencing everyday miracles.

- www.jnutra.com – Your online resource for information and ordering of Dr. Jernigan's frequency-matched remedies and health-related products recommended in his books. Also read about ongoing research and upcoming lay public seminars. Call 877-456-8872.

- www.somerleytoncenter.com – Looking for healing centers that practice the God-Designed healing principles presented in Dr. Jernigan's books and CD's? This is the official website for the healing center that Dr. Jernigan founded, the Somerleyton Center for Biological Medicine. Learn about the staff, services and treatments available and more information on his philosophy of care. More healing centers are going to be opening up across the country. Find the clinic nearest you. Call 316-686-5900.

CPSIA information can be obtained
at www.ICGtesting.com
Printed in the USA
FFOW03n1327010618
46993520-49273FF